Lessons _for_ Your Lunchbox

Soundbites for the soul

Stephen P Rhoades

ISBN: 9798646174124

These articles were originally published in the *Rapid City Journal*, Rapid City, South Dakota and are reprinted with permission of the publisher.

The Happy
Self-Publisher
publish.smile.repeat

www.happyselfpublisher.com

Table of Contents

FOREWORD

I began my coaching career at a very young age of 22 years old when I became the Head Wrestling Coach at Moravian College. I was drawn towards coaching because I loved to compete and had been involved in sports all my life. When I started coaching, I was only six months removed from being coached myself. The bottom line is that I had no idea what I was doing and was eager to grow. I had to keep learning, and that's what I did. I made a stop at Brown University as an assistant and then was fortunate to be named the Head Coach at Harvard University soon after.

As the Harvard Wrestling program climbed the ranks, my desire to win continued to grow, but something was missing. We achieved success quickly, and it felt as if we were just moving from one challenge to the next. In sports, we want results, but to get those results, we need to focus on the process. The athletes need to trust and believe in the process. Later in life, no matter which careers we choose, we hope to keep evolving and striving for success. But at some point, events in our lives force us to evaluate our purpose and our 'why'. Why do we wake up in the morning? Why should anyone care that we do so? All of these thoughts and questions pointed to the need for high character, and I figured out what I was missing. I needed to coach the whole person, not just the athlete.

The first step in coaching the whole person was recruiting the whole person, and especially at a place like Harvard, that meant recruiting high character.

I met Steve Rhoades in 1997 while recruiting his son Brandon to wrestle at Harvard. From the recruiting process, I knew that high character was evident in the entire Rhoades family. At the time, though, I couldn't know the impact Steve would have on me.

As the years progressed, I would randomly get an email from Steve with a small note saying, "check out my latest lesson", which was his Sunday sermon. What Steve didn't know was almost every lesson came at a time when I needed it the most. Whether it was a death in the family, a little pick-me-up, a leadership lesson, or a story that just stopped me in my tracks to take inventory of my own life, Steve's writings consistently pointed me in the right direction.

Jay T. Weiss

David G. Bunning Head Wrestling Coach

Harvard University

LESSONS FOR YOUR LUNCHBOX

As I grow older, I ponder toward my legacy. I realize I was groomed in the age of sound bites. I once came across a book in southern Vermont entitled: "Talk Less, Say More." I never read the book. I didn't have to. The title said it all.

I want to be succinct. In that process I have stumbled upon, retrieved from others and ripped from my soul some truths that I find fruitful. I started by calling them: "Things I Believe In." Eventually, that title gave way to a series of wise one liners, that became "LESSONS FOR YOUR LUNCHBOX".

The following sound bites are "the rod and staff that have comforted me" in my search to have an impact in this world. The statements are short and each one has a story, but for now just ponder them and allow the truth to form your learning.

NEVER DELEGATE A CONFIDENCE: always remember, "and Mary pondered these things in her heart." There are things that I will take to my grave.

WHEN YOU MESS UP—FESS UP: always remember, "Achan hid the fruits of Jericho. He could have avoided his pain with a simple admission." People respect humility over arrogance.

ALWAYS CHOOSE INTEGRITY OVER CONVENIENCE: always remember: "If Aaron would have waited a little longer, he wouldn't have had to eat the ground-up golden calf."

WHILE SAUL IS FALLING, GOD IS CALLING: always remember, "While Saul was being annoying, David was being anointed." Be faithful, your time will come.

WHILE DAVID WAS LEARNING, GOD WAS LOOKING: always remember, "what you do in secret will be rewarded openly."

BE ALERT, BUT NOT ALARMED: always remember, "sheep scatter sheep, and shepherds settle sheep." Jesus said, "In this world you will have tribulation, but be of good cheer, I have overcome the world."

NEVER SAY ANYTHING ABOUT SOMEONE YOU WOULDN'T SAY TO THEM: always remember, "There are ripples to every word you speak, and they strike the shores of life in ways you never dreamed possible."

THERE ARE THINGS YOU NEED TO KNOW AND THINGS YOU WANT TO KNOW: always remember: "a wise leader knows the difference: sometimes it's neither." Jesus said, "It's not for you to know the times or the seasons."

LEADERS ARE LEARNERS: always remember, "Read."

THE HIGHER YOU GO THE FEWER OPTIONS YOU HAVE: always remember, "The position of leader will be judged more strictly."

IT'S TOUGH TO KEEP A FULL CUP STEADY: always remember, "Jesus said: Martha, you are worried and upset about many things, but only one thing is needed." Don't spill your family, your legacy or your soul for the sake of "many things."

THE CLOSER YOU GET THE MORE DIFFICULT IT IS TO CONFRONT: always remember, "Jesus went away by himself for a while," then he faced the problems of those closest to him.

PEOPLE WILL NEVER UNDERSTAND YOUR METHODS UNTIL THEY UNDERSTAND YOUR MOTIVES: always remember, "The Ten Commandments were truths engraved in the heart of Moses by God himself." It's not hard to follow when you know where the vision comes from.

UNLESS YOU ARE BROKEN, YOU WILL NEVER REBUILD: always remember, "Nehemiah bore much sorrow, over his hurting city, long before he rebuilt it." Unless something burdens you enough to break you, it will probably be left in peril. *Until the pain of staying the same becomes greater than the pain of change, men stay the same.*

FOR EVERY BLESSING THERE IS A BOUNDARY: always remember, *"The rules are there to keep the fun in the game."* The Apostle Paul said, "God is not the author of confusion. Everything should be done decent and in order."

FOR EVERY RESTRAINT THERE MUST BE A REASON: always remember, *"Fences are for keeping bad things out and good things in."* The prophet Amos said, "Hate the evil, love the good and stand in judgment at the gate."

BE A VOICE AND NOT AN ECHO: always remember, John the Baptist said: "I am the voice of the one crying in the wilderness." He had his own message.

AND FINALLY, AND MOST IMPORTANTLY…Always remember, "in order to have a decisive legacy, you are certainly going to have to: WRITE YOUR OWN LIST!"

WE CAN'T STAND HERE FOREVER

Acts 20:37: . . . "all the people wept, embraced Paul and kissed him."

Who was it that said: "parting is such sweet sorrow?" I beg to differ with them. That just ain't true. It's all sorrow!!!!!

I cried like a little kid. Well, in many ways I was a little kid. I was only 15, but it was the first time I had ever been away. I decided it was time to step into the world of the independent and try my hand at leaving the nest—one week in the hills of Pennsylvania—five days at camp, away from home. Just think of it, it was the first time my parents had left me alone, and it had to be at a place called, "World's End, Pennsylvania." No mom and dad, no eight brothers and sisters, alone at the end of the world, literally! I cried every night for a week. No amount of comfort could ease my emptiness. All I wanted was that 1972 green Ford Galaxy to come cruising up that dirt lane to take me back to the comforts of my house. Sweet sorrow? I don't think so. Sad scenario? As any good South Dakotan would say, "you betcha!" When the final day of camp arrived, my parents made true on their promise. "We'll be here at the end of the week, have a good time." Sure enough, when Friday came, up the lane they drove. As the old song goes, we were now "reunited, and it feels so good." I never dreamed that someday I would be on the other end of separation anxiety. That day has come and now is!

"We can't stand here forever." I said. "Yeah, that would look kinda dumb, wouldn't it?" was my son's response. A father,

11

mother and son parting ways. Dad and Mom back home to South Dakota, our oldest and only son left behind in Cambridge, Massachusetts for his first year of college. We had just exchanged hugs on Prescott Street looked each other in the eyes and said our goodbyes. Now, we didn't know what to do. We just stood there. Me, wanting to scoop him up along with all his stuff and call off this thing they call growing up. Him hoping that I wouldn't make this too hard or embarrassing.

Sue and I climbed in the "Tracker" and slowly made our way down the street. The "still shot" in the rear-view mirror will be forever etched in my mind. There he went, by himself. He looked so confident. I felt so cold. My friends had told me this wouldn't be easy. Somehow, for me, I thought it would be. We had prepared for this moment. Discussed it over and over. But few things have ever made me feel so empty.

There were a thousand things I wanted to whisper in his ear that day, every one of them legitimate. Now was no time, however, to try and recap eighteen and one-half years of boundaries and building blocks. He was ready. It was time. When it comes to parenting, that's the way it should be. Solomon said: "teach them while they are young, when they are old they won't depart from it." It was too late for a cram session on a crowded Boston street.

The people of Ephesus knew what it was to let their good friend, Paul, go. It was my turn now. Route 90 was a bit blurry for the next couple of hours. I didn't say much until, I think, somewhere around Albany, New York. "You know, Sue, he's ready. He'll be all right. We've done all we can do. He'll be OK We'll just have to let him go," I said. It was time for parting. I guess that's just the way it is. "You can't stand there forever. That would look kinda dumb, wouldn't it?"

REMEMBERING MOM

LOCATION...LOCATION...LOCATION

For those of us who have ever bought a Home, we know that the three most important rules of the process are location... location...location.

When I decided I wanted to say something at Mom's funeral I raced through my mind to cherish all the memories. There were thousands of thoughts and pictures dancing through my brain, but my synapses kept lingering on three of them.

Location #1:

The window: It was a double-paned window in the kitchen at 604 Milltown Road, Wilmington, Delaware this is where she peeled potatoes, breaded chicken, rolled meatballs, made home-made dumplings and also washed a lot of dishes.

Sometime around ninth grade, I noticed that she was spending a little more time at the window than normal. She didn't know it, but you could see her reflection in the window while she was staring out at the trees in the backyard. Her eyes were red, and there was a stream of tears running down her cheeks. I saw it more than once.

One day I finally asked my dad, "Is something wrong with mom?" She cries a lot at the kitchen sink. He looked embarrassed and just said, "No, she's fine." She'll be OK A few days later I asked him again, "Dad, are you sure she is OK?" He had that embarrassed look on his face, like, "Don't make me talk about it." Then he said…"Stephen, its Change of life." I thought, "change of life, what's that?" He said, "it's something ladies go through." That was it. He wasn't going any further.

The next day after Science class, I asked my teacher, "Do you know what change of life means?" He got this little grin on his face and said, "why do you want to know?" I said, "My dad says my mom has it." My teacher responded by saying, "Well, it has a scientific name, it's called menopause." You know what I heard? "Mental Pause." "MENTAL PAUSE?!!!!!" What is that. Now for those of you ladies who get what I'm talking about, you would probably agree that it is kind of a mental pause.

My teacher didn't explain, he just said, "She will get through it, just be nice to her and make sure you behave." The next time I saw my mother's crying reflection in the window I walked up behind her and hugged her and put my face into her hair and kissed her head. I can remember two things about that moment: (1) Her hair smelled like a permanent. My mom got permanents. My sister Carol would put these rollers in her hair and tighten them like a sailor's knot. And that brew she put on her hair smelled and stunk up the whole house. When she was done, Mom's hair would come out like a perfectly shaped ball. It was a permanent. But it wasn't Permanent because several weeks later she had to get another one. They should have called it a temporary. (2) The second thing I remember was her turning toward me, hugging me back, placing her tear wet cheek against my peach fuzz face and whispering, "Thank you, I love you, you are a good boy."

Location #2

The corner of Duncan and McKennan's church Road.

I hated riding the bus to school. It smelled funny, was dirty and I was traveling and singing every weekend and had spent more time in a bus than any 15-year-old should have to. Most mornings I stayed in bed until I heard the most heartwarming words a non-bus rider wants to hear. "Stephen, if you don't get dressed I am going to have to drive you to school." I thought in my mind... "That's the plan." Sometimes I was actually already dressed and laying under the covers until I could hear the muffler of the bus drive away and I would come running like I was on a mission. "Ah, man...missed it again." "Get in the car." She would say. Off we would go in that 1971 Green Ford Galaxy with the vinyl top to the parking lot of Thomas McKean High school.

On this particular morning, it was the day I was going to wrestle Louie Scalia from Delcastle High School. I would have never admitted then, but now that I am old, truth is HE SCARED ME! I knew I was going to lose, and I just wanted to cry.

I must have had a weird look on my face because my mom looked at me and said, "What's the matter?" To which I responded in a heap of tears. I'm scared, I don't want to go to school today and I don't want to wrestle tonight. I'm afraid I am going to lose.

At the corner of Duncan and McKennan's Church Road, my mom sat at a stop sign and leaned over to me and said, "Stephen, do you know what I think of when I look at you? I think this, if anyone can get it done, Stephen can. If I need something done around the house and I need someone strong, I say to myself, Stephen can do it, and you do. Now look at my eyes. This is how I feel about tonight, if anyone can get it done, you can. I believe in you. Don't you be afraid."

15

I felt like Ralphie on the Christmas story, my mom has just believed in me! Yippee, I don't have to be afraid.

That night I rode the team bus from McKean to Delcastle in silent focus. Got ready for the match, listened to Coach Montebell's pre-match speech and went to the mat with confidence. Just before I stepped on the mat, Mr. Montebell pulled me close to his face and said, "Now Steve we all know you're just a sophomore and you are still a little puppy, but I want you to know that I believe you can win this match. Look around this gym, just about everyone in here has said you are going to lose, but me and two other people believe you will win. Look over there in the bleachers, you see your mom and dad, they believe you can win, I believe you can win, and now you go out there and you believe you are going to win." How many of you want to know if I won? Of course, I won; I never tell stories in public about losing.

All because of a pep talk from my mom at the corner of Duncan and McKennan's Church Road.

Location # 3

Church.

It started at 23rd and Pine. Mom and Dad and 8 kids. Every Sunday we would walk up the front steps as a family, dressed to the nines. Shoes tied, shirts tucked, dresses below the knee and hair combed clean to the skin with butch wax. We were cute and we were clean. Quite often this only got accomplished by mom spitting on us. Oh, I don't mean literally, I mean, she would see a spot on our face and she would pull that lace handkerchief out of her purse, lick it and wipe our face with it. It always smelled like breath, not breath mints. BREATH! We had to all sit together, children's church, DIDN'T EXIST. We had to sit, listen, be quiet and not move. If someone acted up, mom would pinch the youngest and say...pass that down to the one in trouble.

About halfway through the service mom would break the great behavior equalizer. A pack of Lifesavers, fruit flavored made the sermons about heaven a little more real because you felt like you were there.

Mom never missed church! When mom and dad went into the ministry she always sat on the front row. Never missed and neither did we. You see, at one time my mom was far from God, she knew what it was to be a lost soul. I always believed my mom sat on the front row because she just never got over being saved. Being forgiven was very important to her and I guess she just never got over it.

Because mom sat in the front row, she had a ring-side seat to everything that went on up on the stage. One time she called to tell me a story of a service in the church on Howell School Road. Dad was leading the singing, Linda was off to the side playing piano and mom was in the front row. As dad was leading he lifted up both his hands and it was just enough to flatten his stomach so that his pants fell down around his ankles. My dad didn't skip a beat. He said, "Every head bowed, every eye closed. No one looking around. God is doing something." At the same time, my mom was laughing so hard she was crying, I heard that my sister Linda lost it too. Dad wiggled (literally) through the moment, got his pants back in order and wore suspenders from then on.

After the service, one of the older ladies in the church came up to mom and said in tears, "Mrs. Rhoades. I love this church.

Pastor Rhoades is so sensitive; he stops the service right in the middle of a song to care for the needy. And while he is doing it, you and your daughter are in tears. Today's service was beautiful. God really moved." To which my mom replied, "Oh God sure did move!"

Location...Location...Location

The window, Duncan and McKennan's Church Road and Church.

Thanks mom for teaching me the three most important rules for life:

1. When other's hurt hug them

2. When others are scared let them know "they can do it!"

3. And when it comes to eternal life, live like you never got over being saved.

ANY OLD STICK WILL DO

Nehemiah 2:4 "And the king said, "What is it you want?"

In the movies we hold our breath for "the moment of truth." At the tire store they say it's "where the rubber meets the road," and on Wall Street they call it "the bottom line." When I was a kid it was playground talk, "it's time to put em' up or shut up!"

Been faced with the bottom line lately? April fifteenth ring a bell? Nehemiah knew what it was to have his own last-minute meeting with the accountant, only to see the big red number at the bottom of the page. He had been waiting four months for this moment and now King Artaxerxes wanted to know what was bothering him.

What would he say? He gulped, shot up a quick prayer and let 13 weeks of pent-up images come spilling out from the depths of his soul.

It was "time to make a change." And he was about to become the agent of change." It was 'put up or shut up." The pain of his ancestors and the embarrassment of his homeland (a city without walls; was no city at all) had gripped his inner being and he wanted to do something about it. And do he did!!!!!!

I kind of know the feeling on a much smaller scale. The lift-gate on my 1992 Plymouth Voyager was broken. Nothing serious, just a two-dollar screw that snapped and broke away from the cylinder that holds the gate open. The other day in the grocery store parking lot, (as I was loading a weeks' worth of grub into the old blue wagon), I looked at that well-worn, cracked broom-handle-turned-cylinder that stood between me and a good conk on the head.

I said to myself, "One of these days that old stick is going to slip and knock you silly." Then I had an even worse thought. "What if it slipped on my wife or one of my daughters and knocked them senseless?" "But the stick is working," I rationalized. Then I had a mental picture: Me in a parking lot, with half of my body stuck out of the back end of the family truckster, yelling for someone to come lift this two-hundred-pound door off my body. Embarrassment made an appointment in my brain, and I made an appointment with Marvin (he fixes my cars)! It is time to replace the stick with something strong.

Artexerxes asked Nehemiah: "What's the problem, and what do want me to do for you?"

Nehemiah responded: "My homeland lays in ruin. It has no walls, and my people are in shame. SEND me home, SECURE me with your blessing, and SUPPLY me with all that I need to finish the job."

For years "any old stick would do" for his hackneyed homeland. For many of us right now "any old stick is doing!" Anything come to mind? I am sure you are envisioning matters far weightier than a two-hundred-pound lift-gate. Family? Finances? Physical problems? Career?

Jesus, on many occasions, said to people of the "any old stick will do" mentality, "What do you want me to do for you?" "It's my sight," one man said. Another with leprosy asked, "Would you make me clean?" And still another queried, "It's my sick child. Would you come and make him better?"

Nehemiah faced the bottom line, knee deep in red ink. King Artexerxes replaced his cracked stick with something strong.

Jesus is a specialist at replacing cracked broom handles holding up heavy doors. He is already asking, "What do you want me to do for you?" Why not trade in your stick and ask for something strong?

FALTERING FOOTWORK

Disaster struck on the third turn before the last lap. Zola Budd tripped up Mary Decker and down she went. Not only did she fall, but her dreams of Olympic greatness, a shot at a gold medal and quite possibly a fortune in endorsements went out the window. Within seconds Olympic officials and her teammates rushed to her side to calm her sorrow, but nothing could stop the tears of disappointment. The dream was not faded; it was gone. The hope of glory was not even a remote possibility. The field had passed her by, and she was left behind huddled in hurt.

In the seventh grade I made my debut in track in the 800 meters. At 4'11" and 88 pounds, I wasn't much of a fearsome foe at the starting line, but Coach Nutter thought this would be the best place for a guy of my expertise. In my first race ever I made it through the first lap and was a long way from first place and an even longer way from the finish line when I noticed a barn on the backstretch. I thought it would be much easier for me to skip the second lap, settle in behind the barn, wait a little while and then walk over to the finish line. I did just that. It couldn't have been more than sixty seconds later when I heard the jingling of keys and a voice calling my name. It was Mr. Nutter. He was holding up his pants with one hand and swinging his belt with the other. "Rhoades, if I find you behind that barn, you've had it." I looked in panic and decided it was time to get back in the race. I hit the track, and he chased me all the way to the finish line. I'm sure that my first lap ranked as one of the slowest in track history, but my second one was close to a world record. When I finished all he said was, "Don't you ever quit on me again." I never did! For me the tripping threats came from burning lungs and coming in last, for Mary Decker Slaney, it was an intruder.

Tripping threats are nothing new. As a matter of fact, hundreds of years ago there was a follower of Christ who understood the problem of outside forces that cause our footsteps to falter. Paul, the apostle, wrote to his friends in a church in Galatia the following words, "You were running a good race. Who cut on you and kept you from obeying the truth?"

What about you? When was the last time someone (or something) cut in on you, knocking you out of the race? Was it a divorce? Abuse? A layoff? A good deal gone bad? Or something else? The list is endless. And the hurt seems just as infinite.

It's time you learned what Mary Decker Slaney and I both learned. "You were called to be free." To run again. To get back in the race.

Have you been knocked off your feet? Why not step back in the race and run to the finish? I think I hear keys jingling.

IGNORE IT OR ADMIT IT

I John 1:9 "If we confess our sins, he is faithful and just and will forgive us our sins and purify us from all unrighteousness."

Day one: 200 athletes arrive at the U.S. Naval Academy in Annapolis, Maryland. 200 wrestlers, who for the next five days would hone their skills with some of America's finest. It was mid-July. Average daily temperatures hovered around 100 degrees. After registration it was orientation and then on to session number one. When that concluded, wringing with sweat, the clothes we wore were hung in our locker to dry.

Day two: Session two. I wore the same clothes as yesterday. They smelled a little, but so did everyone else. You kind of get used to it in a world that begins to stink. Session three was that afternoon, and it was time to break out a new set of workout stuff. This would be the same attire I would wear for tonight's session. That meant tomorrow I would be wearing my last set of apparel. Word spread. There were no washers and dryers. We would all just have to make do.

Day three: Why not just do three sessions in the only clean clothes I had left? By nine o'clock that night my shirt shorts and socks were as wet as a poolside towel. Hang them in the locker. That's what everybody else was doing.

Day four: Everything I had stunk. As a matter of fact, everybody stunk. What do 200 16-year-olds who have never been away from home do with stinky clothes? They revert to what every man has done with his favorite shirt that wasn't washed and ready for wearing. Spray it with Right Guard. Most guys have tried that at least once. It worked. Or so we thought. When we started to wrestle, the whole gym began to emit an odor. To this day, I can still remember the rancid aroma that came from this reeking bunch of wrestlers. We still had two days of wrestling. Six hours of being in close contact with our deodorant-laced clothing. We all at first tried to ignore it. But, eventually, we all had to admit it: "We stunk."

As I contemplated returning home on Friday, I thought it might be just as well if I threw everything away. Mom was never going to get this stuff to smell good again. She also wasn't going to be too happy when she opened the plastic garbage bag that I had borrowed from a friend to haul this stuff. When I pulled in the driveway after four hot hours on the road, everybody came out to welcome me. I told my little brother to grab the big green garbage bag and take it to the laundry room. He did. It sat there until Monday.

It was sometime Monday morning when Mom started the wash for the week, that she opened my bag. I could have heard my name from three blocks away as she screamed, "Steeeeephen.! What is in this bag!!? It smells like a dead rat laced with Right Guard!" Oh well, she was close.

I ran to the basement and told her the whole story. She understood and graciously had *ME* put them in the washer while she stood back and walked me all the way through the spin cycle.

Later that afternoon, when I returned from work, there was a pile of freshly washed workout clothes at the foot of the steps. I picked them up, held them to my nose, and couldn't believe they were the same threads. They were rosy fresh—just what every wrestler wants his clothes to smell like.

I learned something in that week of adolescence. When you spray fresh-smelling deodorant on sour-smelling clothes, "until they get washed we're just kidding ourselves!"

Too much sweat with no place to get clean leads to a pretty smelly lifestyle. In the same vein, too much sin and never taking time to pray makes us all a little foul. Does that sound like the way your life has been going lately? Sin makes us all stink. When it does, the Bible gives us directions on how to become clean all over.

Confess your sins! Jesus will forgive you.

By the way, when sending your kids to camp, pack some extra clothes. They'll be glad you did; and in the end, you'll be glad you did.

IN OVER MY HEAD

And David cried: "My soul is full of trouble and my life draws near the grave." Psalm 88:3

"That's right, down and back four times." Those were the words of Mr. Emerick, my tenth grade Phys. Ed. Teacher. It didn't seem like much, just 100 yards of freestyle swimming. We had been working on our strokes. Today, we put them to the test. I had always risen to the occasion, and this wouldn't be any different.

Into the pool I went, ready for what I considered to be just another grade in his little red book. Swim for a while, get out of the pool and head for my next class.

After one lap I could see out of the corner of my eye that I wasn't in first place, but I wasn't in last place either. Lap two; I felt a tight twinge in my side. I kept going, but it hurt. I wanted to quit. Quitting, however, was not in my vocabulary. The pack had passed me, and I was in the place I promised myself I would never be, especially in gym class: DEAD LAST. I made the turn and headed for the deep end of the pool. Within moments I experienced something that I had never felt before and could not explain. My body started sweating, and my eyes filled with tears. I was in a cold pool, yet my skin got all clammy. I had just crossed into the danger zone, when I couldn't go any further. I was experiencing, for the first time, a panic attack. I stroked like crazy, cried out for help and started going under.

My teacher came running, jumped in the pool, grabbed me under both arms and became my deep-end deliverer. The rest of the class sat staring at me. Mr. Emerick asked me if I would be OK. I didn't answer. For the first time in my life, I wasn't sure if I would be OK or not. The class dismissed, and this teacher became my friend. "What happened?" He asked. "I just got scared. I was afraid I wasn't going to be able to make it out of the deep end. I panicked!" That was the first time I was in over my head, but it for sure wasn't the last. Here's the short list of some of my deep-end experiences: A layoff, college English, 16 months with two mortgages, Dad's death, and at age 29 having my zeal pass my abilities while leading a church full of people. The list goes on, but I think you get the message. Uptight and full of tears. Going under, and in need of a friend.

There once was a little girl who was terrified of thunderstorms. Every time the thunder would clap in the night, she would come running into Mommy and Daddy's bedside. One night Dad took her back to her room, tucked her in bed, and said, "Don't worry about the storm, honey. God is with you." The little girl looked up through tear-veiled eyes and said, "I know that, Daddy, but tonight I need someone with skin."

Do you know someone whose soul is full of trouble? Is their life near the grave? Are they in over their head? As Samuel Taylor Coleridge once said, "Friendship is a sheltering tree." David's trees came from the hall of fame of the unfamiliar. Ittai, Zadok, Abiathar, Hushai, Shobi, Machir and Barzillai. Not exactly faces that will be gracing the cover of a Wheaties box anytime soon, but deep-end deliverers, they were.

What about you? Have you gotten wet lately?

LAST WORD'S

"And Jesus said to Peter, 'Follow Me!'" John 21:19

Somewhere between a cool October canoe ride on Lake George in upstate New York and the sterile smells of an eighth-floor intensive care unit lies the last words of a dying man.

Last words say a lot about a person. Take Jesus, for example. His last words to his beloved friend, Peter (who had once left him high and dry in the courtyard), were, "Follow me."

Or how about Clarence Darrow? Joseph Stowell in his book, "Following Christ," tells Darrow's story this way: "...John Herman, who had earned two PhDs, had a lifelong ambition to meet the brilliant criminal lawyer, Clarence Darrow, who had become famous in the 'Scope's Monkey Trial.' Late in Herman's life it was arranged for the two men to meet. Sitting in the attorney's living room, Herman asked Darrow, 'Now that you've come this far in life and you're not doing much lecturing, teaching or writing anymore, how would you sum up your life?' Without hesitation Darrow walked over to a coffee table and picked up a Bible. This took his guest by surprise since Darrow was an atheist who spent much of his life ridiculing Scripture. 'This verse in the Bible describes my life.' Darrow turned to the fifth chapter of Luke, the fifth verse. He changed the 'we' to 'I'. 'I have toiled all night and taken nothing.'

He closed the Bible, put it back on the coffee table, and looked Herman straight in the face. 'I have lived a life without purpose, without meaning, without direction. I don't know where I came from. And I don't know what I'm doing here. And worst of all, I don't know what's going to happen to me when I punch out of here.'

Your last words can forever speak your legacy.

While enjoying the humdrum of paddling my two toddlers around a small island on Lake George, my wife received a message that I was to call home. Not the home where I was raising my family, but to Delaware where my Mommy and Daddy raised me. I called, and my brother said, "I think you should come home. Daddy's had a stroke, and he isn't doing so good." Within the hour we were headed back to my roots.

When I arrived, it was far worse than I imagined. Dad's face was twisted, his speech slurred, and the whole left side of his body paralyzed. I tried like crazy to hold back my grief. The strong man of my youth laid crippled and confined. Through slurred words and stuttering we caught up on old times. He spoke as if nothing had happened. He was being himself as I struggled to keep from screaming. He told me of his upcoming therapy, how he was going to walk again, that his speech would come back, and that it wouldn't be long before he would be going home.

I stayed for a while and told him that I would be there to help Mom and him. Then I said goodbye and headed for the door. As I got to the foot of his bed; he called my name. I turned to see what he wanted. His eyes were filled with tears. With scrambled speech he said: "Stephen, you're a good man." I went back and hugged him one more tearful time.

That was Tuesday. On Thursday he had another stroke and that Saturday he died. I didn't know it at the time, but they were his last words to me.

What will your last words be? "I have toiled all night and taken nothing?" Or "You're a good man?" You decide.

YOU DON'T LOSE IT; YOU USE IT

MATTHEW 5:5 "Blessed are the MEEK, for they shall inherit the earth"

Last year I started early and indoors. Seven flats full of new seeds. Pumpkins, radishes, squash, peppers, cucumbers and even watermelons. Artificial light adorned the shelf in my homemade hothouse. Mr. Green Thumbs was off and running. I watered and watched as seedlings sprouted and color filled the flats. In the process of getting my gardening going, I never dreamed that I would learn the truth about meekness.

Colleen Townsend-Evans led me into a deeper understanding of the word "meek." It means "to arrange in order, like the rows of a garden, to act in a suitable or proper manner." The meaning eventually was translated, "soft and gentle." When the word used to describe an animal, it means "a wild animal that has been tamed." One no less strong, but whose strength has been channeled and made usable.

When "meek" is used to describe a human being, it refers to a person who has been settled or quieted, particularly after anger. This is not a weak person. This is a strong-spirited individual who has been tamed—molded—by God. He no longer flies off in all directions; he has direction. Neither is his spirit broken. With God working through him, he is stronger than ever.

Meekness means "strength," but not raw power that may strike out and destroy. Meekness is gentle power. "It builds, it lifts up, it restores."

Have you ever heard of a person, who's behavior consistently gets out of control, say, "I can't help it; I just lose my temper. That's just the way I am?" When I hear that statement, my response is always the same. I ask a question.

"Have you ever been pulled over by a policeman when you were driving?" {Most people can relate to that (I know I can).} The response is an overwhelming, "Yes." I then ask another question, "When that happened, did you fly off the handle and tell the policeman what a pain in the neck this was going to cause you? Scream at him, lose your cool and threaten him?" Again, the response is an overwhelming, "No." I then get to the point. "Then under certain conditions, you can control yourself. Right?" Usually, this is met with, "But that is different. That's a policeman." To which I respond, "Oh, and the policeman deserves more respect than those we love?" By this time the point is beginning to find roots.

I close this conversation on un-meekness with the following statement, "You don't lose your temper, you just use your temper."

A keen understanding of meekness makes us aware that this is a gift for all of us. Who among us doesn't want a "well ordered life?" A broken horse contributes much more to life than a wild stallion. Energy out of control is dangerous; energy under control is powerful.

Robert Hagar, a reporter for MSNBC, shares the following report from the 1979 disaster at Three Mile Island in Harrisburg, Pennsylvania.

For NBC I had been in Vietnam, Northern Ireland and the Iranian Revolution. But this was a different sort of threat. Radioactive, invisible and silent. The sirens, it turned out, had sounded because there had just been a new release of radiation into the air (though, by later analysis it did not seem to present a major threat at ground level.) A valve at the plant had been opened for several hours because of a new pressure buildup.

On that word, Pennsylvania Gov. Richard Thornburgh had urged pregnant women and pre-school children within a five-mile radius of the plant to leave, ordered 23 schools closed and advised people over a broad area of central Pennsylvania to remain indoors if they could. Meantime, the Nuclear Regulatory Commission was warning that, ultimately, the time might come when everyone should evacuate.

The incident set the tone for the nation over the next several days. The enemy was a hydrogen bubble, growing inside the dome of the plant's reactor. The bubble, in turn, was a consequence of overheating that had severely damaged the core of the plant's radioactive fuel. The fear was that there could be a complete meltdown, or that the pressure of the bubble could burst the dome. Either scenario would release huge amounts of radioactivity into the air or soil, and potentially bring devastation to millions of people."

Energy out of control is chaos. Meekness or Tameness is energy under control.

Jesus took Matthew, a suave, tricky politician, who knew the political ropes well enough to keep from dangling from one—

and, putting the bridle of grace upon him, changed him into an agent of blessing.

Seven seedling flats, all arranged in order, slowly growing roots in my downstairs nursery. Meekness ready for the challenge of the outdoors. "How did my garden grow?", you may ask. That's a story for another day.

MOLLY

"To be frivolously minded brings death, but to be morally minded is life and peace." *(Romans 8:6)*

She was 40 pounds of playful puppy, and that was when she was but a wee one...a slippery, slimy, slobbery, Saint Bernard. Molly was our pet, the neighborhood bundle of puppy love. There were nine of us kids in the Rhoades clan, all of which thought Molly was the ultimate "man's best friend."

We taught her to wrestle, literally. I mean moves and all. She was charming and chubby. Well-fed and well bred. She made coming home a whole new adventure.

The concrete path to our garage became known as the driveway of doom. The jingle of her dog tags was a friendly reminder to take cover or get run over. If I was up for it (or not), she would attack, usually at my feet. Down I would go and then it was off for a five-minute grappling session with "Beethoven." Slobber went everywhere. There was licking and grabbing, pushing and pulling. When I was totally exhausted, she still wanted more. She was as playful as she was powerful. The way to end it all was to escape into the house for a good bath.

But Molly had a problem. You see, she just wouldn't grow up. We paid for training. We brought in friends that were experts in the field of obedience, but she just never seemed to catch on. At first (as with most of the dogs in our suburban section of town), we let her roam free with her friends (a couple of German shepherds and a beagle). They were buds. But problems loomed "large" on the horizon. As she grew older, the damage increased. It went from a few flowerbeds crushed under the weight of a man-sized scratcher, to several garbage cans torn hither and yon. The neighbors were in a dither, and our dog would have to go "on the leash."

We started with a corkscrew-type restraint that twisted into the ground. It didn't last long. The next day, when I pulled into the driveway arriving home from church, Molly came running. The chain and corkscrew were dangling from her neck like a 70s peace sign. Up she went, and down I dropped. It was no time to play. I was left with spit and muddy paw prints on my Sunday best.

Dad began to suggest that we get rid of Molly. Perish the thought! She was a Rhoades, and we would see this thing through. All she needed was a new set of boundaries. We bought her a bigger doghouse, ran a huge eyehook through the frame and hooked it to her leather necklace. Our monster, "Molly," was now safe. Or so we thought.

One crisp fall morning in my junior year of high school, I had to ride the cheese bus (my 68 Pontiac was in for repairs). As we were leaving my stop, the kids started craning through the crowd to look out the windows. With my eyes still straining to free themselves from sleepers, I looked, too. Here came Molly, dragging a 120 pound dog house down Rural Route Number Two. It was hilarious. The bus driver was laughing so hard she had to stop old "Cheeser." Molly was going to school with a backpack the size of Rhode Island.

My bus driver gave me a reprieve. I drug our charming chubby friend and her domicile back into our yard and hoped she would understand. I told her to stay, and she did—long enough for me to get around the corner and our bus driver to wipe the tears of laughter from her eyes.

Within a few days, as I arrived home from soccer practice, I extricated myself from my ugly tan Pontiac, prepared myself for a pounding, and headed for the big oak tree that was now Molly's margin maker. It seemed like we just had to keep going to something bigger and stronger to keep her from blowing it.

I didn't hear any jingling. I couldn't see those big dirty paws prepared to seal my doom to dirtdom. I was sure she had run off again. I walked into the house, only to be met by the tearful eyes of my younger siblings. Mom said sorrowfully, "Molly's gone. She broke her chain and met her fate at the hands of the garbage truck. Dad had to take her to be 'put to sleep.'" I sat down and cried, and went through the list of "if only's," trying to diminish the disappointment.

You see, Molly had the same problem many people have. They seem charming enough. They mean no harm, and surely, if given the chance, they would show you their playful side. If we could only keep them from drinking, or get them to stay off drugs. Convince them to keep their paws out of someone else's stuff. Sometimes they make us laugh, like the day the big brown and white slobber machine pulled her townhouse down the highway. But eventually, they always seem to make us cry.

We try bigger and stronger boundaries, anything to keep them safe. Unfortunately, boundary breakers are sure they can handle it. Life becomes a spiraling spin into the world of "living on the ragged edge." Eventually, they take a trip to where the garbage lies, and we get the bad news: "they have reached the end of their rope."

If you find yourself, like Molly, stretching the limits all in the name of harmless hoopla, you may be headed for a tragedy. It will leave Mom, Dad, and the whole family sitting in tears. The fate of Molly awaits those who won't exercise restraint. For the sake of us all, stop straying. We love it when you leave mud on our Sunday best.

MUSCLES

James 1:3 "The trying of your faith develops perseverance."

Racks of iron in a sweaty gym, old plastic weights in the corner of a basement and high-tech machines at the local fitness club, all means to amassing muscles. But bulky biceps, titanic triceps and colossal calf's aren't born overnight. There is just no way to quickly form a favorable physique. Even one-named heroes like, "Arnold, Stallone, Tarzan, and Holyfield," had to do their fair share of pumping iron before they displayed their sculptured structures.

Now that doesn't mean we might not try to skirt the rule of hard work. For instance…several years ago my only son, a first grader at the time, was taking his Saturday bath (not that he didn't take baths at other times during the week). After he was finished, my wife, Susan, went in to drain the tub and noticed that all of the shampoo was gone. That was strange, because it was a brand new bottle. She really didn't think too much about it and went on with her night.

After Brandon was in his pajamas, he came into the family room acting rather strange. He kept staring at his biceps and giggling. So we giggled, too. Sometimes just watching a six-year-old acting weird can make you laugh. I finally said, "Son, what's so funny?" He just kept laughing. So we kept laughing. Finally he said: "Do my muscles look any bigger?" I said, "Well, they look a little bigger (although in reality they were still the lanky arms of a first grader)." He laughed again. "What's so funny?" I said. He said, "Come here." And then he led me to the bathroom, picked up the empty bottle of shampoo and shared some insight into why he was acting so strange. "Dad, I took this whole bottle of shampoo and put it all over my body. I am feeling a lot bigger. Can you tell? See it says right here: 'BODY BUILDING FORMULA!'"

What a hoot! I thought I was going to slip a disk I laughed so hard. Susan lost it, too. He even laughed. When we gained our senses, we explained the entire process of hair care to him, and then politely asked him to refrain from trying to become Arnold Schwarzenegger overnight at our expense. As far as we know, he laid off the shampoo regime, and since then every muscle is "au natural!"

There is no easy way to be strong and consistent. It is as testing is endured that our relationship with Christ is more durable. James says, "The testing of your faith produces "perseverance." The word he uses for *"perseverance"* can best be translated *"toughness."*

R. Kent Hughes in his study on James states: "Here is how this works: we develop toughness or fortitude by repeatedly being tested and 'prevailing.' The more tests we pass, the tougher we become. The endurance and fortitude of the Apostle Paul, Billy Graham or Corrie ten Boom did not come overnight, and it was not developed apart from trials. Paul, in Romans 5:3, confirms this truth: 'But we also rejoice in our sufferings, because we know that suffering produces perseverance.'

Nature teaches us this principle. Free a butterfly from its chrysalis, and thus from the struggle of liberating itself, and you destroy its life, for it will never develop the strength to soar as it should. When fortitude is lacking in one of his children,

God has a time-tested remedy—'the testing of your faith.' With this in mind James' irrational call to 'consider it pure joy, my brothers, whenever you face trials of many kinds'—becomes brilliant."

Are you being tested lately? Consider it an opportunity to become tougher. Toughness only comes over time. You can't squeeze this element of perseverance out of some plastic bottle during a Saturday night bath. That kind of strength is only found in the fairy tales of first graders.

POOLING PENNIES FOR PERFUME

Proverbs 31:8 "Her children arise and call her blessed...."

Affordability and diversity. They were the determining factors in Mother's Day gifts. However, the range in both categories were "slim and two." In a family of 9 children, the weekly allowance consisted of three squares and a roof over our heads. Outlays of cash were few and far between!

When Mother's Day arrived, the common procedure was a pooling of pennies and a request for Mom to drop us off at the local shopping center. For, the next few hours we walked the sidewalks hoping to outdo last year's purchase. After treks through jewelry stores, Penny's, and Sears, inevitably, we wound up at Old Faithful—Woolworth's.

The whole brood would wander the aisles hoping to stumble upon a treasure for less than five bucks, but each year the consensus would steer us back to the front counter for another gaze at our old standby. Our wallet and the front counter had two things in common, Prince Machiavelli or Evening In Paris. The toughest decision on those warm Saturdays was which incredible fragrance we would bless our mother with tomorrow.

We made our purchase right before Mom picked us up at the back entrance to Sears. As we hid our prize all the way home, we'd play twenty questions to see if she could guess what we had come up with. Although I think she knew all along that it was one of the two affordable fragrances we gave her every year, she never once said either of their names. She kept the surprise alive.

When we arrived home, we scurried to find wrapping paper (sometimes it was yesterday's newspaper), wrapped it as best we could, then hid the purple bottle somewhere that Mom would never look.

The next morning before church, out came the gift and up went Mother's praise. She splashed a little on, and out the door we flew. The whole way there we could smell Mom's new fragrance and feel the joy of giving from a poor man's wallet.

I don't think they make those fragrances any longer, but I'm sure if they did, I would recognize them. That aroma would bring back warm visions of Mom's loving acts. Homemade spaghetti and meatballs, chicken pot pie, warm hugs and encouraging words. You may not believe this, but the thought of Evening In Paris still makes me think of how much Mom loved me and the ways she proved it.

At 72 pounds in seventh grade, I probably wasn't much of a threat to the competition. But in my mother's eyes, I was an athlete. I didn't look like one. My wrestling uniform was three sizes too big. The straps were gathered at my shoulders and held tight with athletic tape. We couldn't afford real wrestling shoes, so my P.F. Flyers were secured tightly to my feet with more athletic tape. How I looked didn't matter to Mom. She was my biggest fan. And she never missed my matches.

It didn't snow often in my hometown, but the day of my first official wrestling match we got whacked with several inches. There was some question as to whether our meet would be canceled, but the coaches and officials decided to stay on schedule.

I knew Mom wouldn't be able to attend because we only had one car, and Dad was out of town.

Adorned in my mummified uniform, I joined the team in the locker room to prepare for the pre-match rituals just before it was time to run out around the mat to warm up. Every ounce of adrenaline that could be produced by a 72-pound weakling was pumping through my veins. I was the first one out the door. Running full speed, I spied Mom out of the corner of my eye sitting in the second row of the bleachers. I remember seeing her rubber see-through boots (with the little elastic eye hook that held them tight to keep out the snow) still on her feet. Mom was here! As I peered her direction to make sure she could see me, suddenly, my feet hit the curled-up edge of a wrestling mat that had been in storage all winter. I went flying, which caused the rest of the team to cascade into a helpless heap. I was so embarrassed. That was the last day I went out of the locker room first.

My first match wasn't exactly an Olympic performance. I lost 17-2 and got turned every which way but loose. But it didn't seem to matter to Mom. She just wiggled through three periods of me fighting off my back, and walked back home smiling proudly.

I learned something valuable that day: "Whether I won or lost, it had no effect on how much my mother loved me!"

It wasn't a stretch for me to give all I had for a purple bottle of perfume. A snow-soaked mother made it all worthwhile.

QUESTIONS

Psalm 23

Forgive me for getting personal, but the very fact that I am writing on QUESTIONS reveals the reality that I have asked a few questions of my own, AND SO DO YOU. It was at one of the lowest points of my life that I learned an amazing principle that turned me toward a deeper and stronger relationship with God than ever before.

You see, I come from three generations of people of Christian faith. Over the years they taught me to "TRUST AND OBEY." Not to say that is wrong, it just seemed to ring hollow. At this moment in time, I was dealing with my own mortality and trying to balance the doubts I had with the faith of the pillars of my heritage. Let me explain.

I can remember it like yesterday. I was only 30 years old when I got the news that my father (who was a pastor) had a stroke and wasn't going to make it. Within two weeks the man who cheered at all my soccer games and wrestling matches for the past 18 years, the man who had been my biggest fan, was gone.

I kept telling myself that the Bible says, "to be absent from the body is to be present with the Lord." That worked for a while until one day I was sitting in my office preparing to preach my ninth funeral in the 4 months that followed my father's death. The depression was so heavy I couldn't stand it anymore. I was reduced to tears and heaving sobs. I sat there knowing that in a few hours I would have to stand before another grieving family. It was important to me that the preacher be composed. My image didn't allow for the minister to struggle.

I called my wife, who knew my inner conflict, and told her I was doing poorly that day and didn't know if I could do this funeral. She said, "Let your assistant take it. People will understand. You've been through too much, you need to give it a break." To which I responded, "I hear you, honey, but what will I say when people ask what is wrong? I'm the preacher. You know it's the reality of scripture that is the source of my struggle. I can't be that vulnerable and survive. I'm just going to go on. When I'm done today, I'm coming home, and we'll take a walk."

I hung up the phone and went back to work, but something had changed. The light came on. It's OK for the faithful to flounder. It's OK for the image conscious to drop their guard. I was still in despair, but, as I would learn later, I was turning my theology into my biography. It was then, and only then, that I felt a new beginning. I could ask God questions, and He could handle them. I'm still asking questions. I guess you would say that is mostly what I do.

Questions caused me to become like the little girl in Sunday School who was asked by the teacher to come to the front of the room and recite the 23rd Psalm. She slowly went to the head of the class, stood on a box at the podium and quietly spoke the following words: "THE LORD IS MY SHEPHERD, THAT'S ALL I WANT," and turned and went to her seat.

When it comes to questions, I can assure you that if "THE LORD IS YOUR SHEPHERD, AND HE'S ALL YOU WANT," you will find He can handle your uneasiness. Go ahead and ask questions.

I can tell you from experience that "when you come to the end of yourself, you come to the beginning of God."

RIVERS, RAFTS, AND RATS

"So, Caleb said, 'I was forty years old when Moses sent me to explore the land. On that day Moses swore to me the land on which my feet had walked. The Lord has kept me alive for forty-five more years, and I am still as strong today as I was then. Now give me the hill country that was promised to me.'"
(Joshua Chapter 14)

At age forty, he was a spy. He led the life of an ancient Navy Seal, carrying out covert action behind Canaan's enemy lines. Now, at 85, he wanted to be a land developer. The time had arrived for this tough senior citizen to request his reward. This no-nonsense member of the AARP slapped down his membership card in front of Joshua and said: "I have come to lay claim to my benefits!"

Caleb reminds me of a seasoned John the Baptist. Kind of a "locust, wild honey, leather belt and Camel's hair jacket" kinda guy. In our day he might ride a Harley, wear a leather jacket (a lot more comfortable than Camel's hair), and set up a ministry at the Sturgis Rally. Quite possibly he would enjoy the outdoors: rock climbing, Ironman Triathlons, ATV's, or maybe he would be a river rat.

Every river has its rats, you know? Not literal rats. I mean river rats. People who ride the river and know every rock and rapid. They live for the rush of rip tides and usually end up riding shotgun on a big rubber raft. It's easy to identify a river rat: beard, strong arms, good tan, a few scars from battles lost with

Mother Nature, and of course, a camel hair jacket. River rats may not be big on presentation, but they are long on dedication.

It's not hard to find a river rat. They live at the Grand Canyon kayaking down the Colorado. There are others in Jackson Hole, literally snaking down the Snake. I heard about one who rafted down the Youghiogheny, a river that runs from West Virginia up through the edge of Maryland and on into Pennsylvania. At times this body of water is a raging torrent, fit only for river rats and crazies who want to prove one more time that you can endure life on the edge and live to tell your story.

My best friend, Jim (a true river rat), faced this river every year at high water. Each time he invited five friends to go bouncing and bumping for six hours. It was their annual attempt to cheat life for a day. On this trip the lead rat screamed things like, "Dig right, dig left, paddle, paddle, paddle, HANG ON!!!!" Being able to remain in the boat was the first rite of passage in becoming an apprentice river rat.

Upon Jim's return, the stories were staggering. Grown men fingernail deep in Gore-Tex and rubber. Six dads now joined together into the "royal order of the river rat."

Caleb would have signed up for that trip. He enjoyed life. He wasn't jaded by forty years of wondering in the wasteland desert with a multitude of whining weaklings. He wasn't disillusioned by the fact that his whole generation of friends had died off before they could enjoy grape clusters so big that it took two men to carry them.

When he was fingernail deep in manna and quail during those forty-five years, he just kept pushing toward the promise, as he silently heard God saying, "Dig right, dig left, paddle, paddle, paddle, HANG ON!!!!"

Dr. Ken Dychtwald in his book, "The Age Wave," gives us some insightful information concerning the times in which we live, including the real possibility that many of us will someday stand where Caleb stood.

"The census bureau projects that by the year 2040 life expectancy will be 75 years for men and 83 for women. To sum all this up in a little over 200 years America has experienced a doubling in the life expectancy of its population. For the first time in our history, we are experiencing a mass society of healthy, active elders."

I have yet to ride the raging waters of the Youghiogheny, but, as Tennessee Ernie Ford used to say, "Good Lord willin' and the creek don't rise," someday I will. What promise are you waiting for? Stay in the boat. It may be a while, but "oh those grapes!"

SINGING IN THE RAIN!

Psalm 126:5-6 "Those who sow in tears will reap with songs of joy. He who goes out weeping, carrying seed to sow, will return with songs of joy, carrying sheaves with him."

In 1932 a man was walking across the desert, stumbling, almost dying of thirst, when on the horizon, he saw a well. As he approached the well, he found a note in a can close by. The note read: "Dear friend, there is enough water in this well, enough for all, but sometimes the leather washer gets dried up and you have to prime the pump. Now if you look under the rock just west of the well, you will find a bottle of water, corked. Please don't drink the water. What you've got to do is take the bottle of water and pour the first half very slowly into the well to loosen up the leather washer. Then pour the rest in very fast and pump like crazy! You will get water. The well has never run dry. Have faith. And when you're done, don't forget to put the note back, fill up the bottle and put it back under the rock. Good luck, have a fun trip. Sincerely, your friend, Desert Pete."

What would you do? You're on the verge of expiring from lack of water, and in reality the bottle of water is only enough to quench your thirst, not save your life. Would you have the courage to risk it all?

This story is a powerful allegory about some of the essential ingredients in the Christian faith. First there is evidence—there is a written message, the can with the letter in it and the bottle underneath the rock. Everything is in order, but there is no proof that you can trust Desert Pete. The second element is risk. Here is a man dying of thirst asked to pour the only water he is sure of down a dark hole in the ground. The third element is work. Some people have mistakenly interpreted faith as a substitute for work. Faith is not laziness. Desert Pete reminds us that after we trust and risk, we must pump like crazy.

In Burkina Faso, West Africa, you will find the literal fulfillment of Psalm 126. The people of this poor country have to sow when the rainy season comes. When they finally reap the harvest of their labor, they save one small bag of seed and hang it in the hut that they call home. As the year progresses, the supply of family food slowly dwindles. The children become hungry, and their bellies begin to swell. Mothers and fathers cut back on the amount of food every family member is allowed to eat until all are slowly starving.

A friend told me of a story of a Burkinabe child who was curiously hunting around the hut when he discovered the little sack of grain hanging behind a picture frame. The excited little fella came running to his father and with excitement holds out the tiny sack and joyfully says, "Oh Papa, here is grain! We can have a great feast." The sad-faced father, through tears, looks down at his starving child and begins to tell him that this grain is reserved for next year's harvest. He explains that if the weather cooperates and the soil is good, the family will have food after the rains come. Quietly and sullenly, the father returns next year's hope to the hook behind the family picture.

As the rainy season approaches, the father takes his little boy upon his back, walks out into the field and slowly plants the seed. As he drops his grain along the ground, tears begin to flow from his eyes; because he knows that what he is planting by faith could feed his child now, but if it grows, it will feed them for another year. As he plants he prays. Daddy sows in tears, but in few months, by faith, he believes, he'll be "singing in the rain."

What would you do? Your whole family is at death's door, and your little one comes to you with eyes of promise. Would you be willing to hang the sack back where it belongs, plant later and pray for a downpour?

Dessert Pete and the Burkinabe father understand what it means to take a step of faith. One pours a bottle of water down a pitch-black hole, the other drops his seeds into some shoddy soil. But both walk away with a song. Sowing in tears is no easy step, but the Psalmist has also said, "I was young, and now I am old, yet I have never seen the righteous forsaken or their children begging bread." Today may be your day to pour some water or plant some seed. Always remember: pour and pump, plant and pray. Before long, you'll be singing in the rain.

SURVIVING THE FAMILY CALAMITY

Genesis 7:6 "Noah was six hundred years old when the floodwaters came on the earth. Noah and his sons and his wife and his sons' wives entered the ark to escape the waters of the flood."

Sometimes I ought to just leave those leadership journals sitting on the shelf! One day after reading one, I came home from my office and told my wife that the latest copy of "Preacher Today" said that every dad that was worth his salt should take his family on a camping trip. Of course, my mind went immediately to that lot down the highway that rented motor homes with all the amenities. A veritable house on wheels. But the author of the article said "this family adventure" needs to be one where our creature comforts meet the rustic road. Tents, firewood, s'mores and sleeping bags. This had to be the real thing. I conceded (which was a real switch, since I always said, "my idea of camping was a Holiday Inn without an indoor pool")..

Our children were seven and five. I made the announcement, and they got pumped. Dad in a tent. Bugs, snakes, chipmunks and sleeping on the ground. A family of four in a three-man tent. I didn't even own my own sleeping bag (still don't). I went to the basement, pulled out Brandon and Erin's tent (a three-man tent we had purchased with green stamps, (ask your grandma), gathered up blankets, fresh fire wood, cut coat hangers to cook hot dogs and marshmallows over the fire, then stuffed a cooler full of camping food. We were ready. After we had all our gear packed in the "second car" (a 1988 Pontiac T1000 compact, two doors and four seats), off to "Red Rock Mountain, Pennsylvania" we went. The kids singing songs and me asking questions. How do you set up a tent, so it doesn't blow away? Are you really allowed to have a fire outside? What if I can't sleep? What if we don't fit? It must have been an interesting scene, me smiling at the kids in the rear view, all the while my city slicker's soul squirming inside my head.

How come I didn't come home and say, "Hey, let's set the tent up in the family room, eat popcorn from the microwave, make milkshakes and watch the 'Brady Bunch' on T.V.?" They would have gone for it, and I would have met the standards of full-fledged fatherhood.

I am convinced to this day that although my wife was gung-ho on this whole idea on the outside, she was laughing herself to tears on the inside. "Stephen sleeping in a tent? This should be good."

We arrived at Red Rock, paid the customary fine (I mean fee), found our site and unpacked. The children were already feeding the live animals peanuts when it hit me, "What if it rains?" Perish the thought. God would never subject me to a punishment like that.

After four hours of stories, s'mores, snacks and a stroll through the woods, it was time to settle in.

I know they were watching. Who? You may ask. Who was watching? You know, Eddie Bauer and Mr. Coleman. The guys on the sites next to us. Grown men with families camping in 35-foot houses on wheels. I could just hear them saying: "Honey, look. Remember when we used to do that? Boy, am I glad those days are over!" They had to be watching. A family of four sleeping in a green-stamp tent. Well, at least we were good entertainment.

Off to bed we went. Four little people tucked in a little red tent, wrapped up in a pile of blankets that would remind you of Joseph's coat of many colors.

We were long since settled when it hit. The thing we feared had come upon us. First the sound of a few little splattering drops hitting the side of our shelter from the storm. Within minutes, the whole sky cut loose. I held Susan close, and she said, "Don't worry, Honey. Everything will be all right." After about 35 minutes of torrential downpour we felt it. The family camper had sprung a leak. No, not just a leak, our green stamp shelter had become a sponge. We did all we could to fend off Mother Nature, but there was no way out. The old "tentster" just wasn't going to cut it. We were swamped, the blankets now weighed 35 pounds apiece, and I was facing the question that every seasoned woodsman has asked himself, "What do we do now?"

At that point in my life there was only one thing that I hated more than camping and that was "giving up." I looked over at Susan, and gathered up my two offspring. I flipped down the rear seat of the Pontiac, grabbed the dry clothes we had left in the car, made a bed in the back and told her we would be sleeping in the reclining buckets. This storm wasn't going to beat us. I was determined—no motel was going to suck up our family fun.

I'm sure we looked a bit odd. Can you picture it? Bauer and Coleman next door in their Winnebago's watching the ball game and eating marshmallow cookies, when out of the corner of their eye they see "tentman" and his family of four sleeping in a compact.

Embarrassing? Yes. Me, quit? Never. A good challenge doesn't destroy a true woodsman.

Are you facing a family calamity? If not, don't worry, you will. Noah did. It is obvious that his story wasn't all that funny, but he did survive! Why? Because he didn't quit.

THE BUMPS ARE WHAT YOU CLIMB ON

"Jonathan climbed up the cliffs of Bozez and Seneh, using his hands and feet, with his armor bearer right behind him. It was then that the Philistines fell before him." I Samuel 14:1-14

Let's face it, we all have our cliffs to climb. We preachers have a perspective on cliff climbing that few people encounter. It is enhanced when we are called to comfort.

There are two rooms that always cause me to breathe a silent prayer before I enter. When I get to the door of this duet that has become the setting for the struggling, the disclosures are rarely delightful. Often I find myself hesitant to enter, concerned that my humanity may be too anemic to overcome the ravages of reality. Sometimes I feel like nothing I say will bring help to the hurting and hope to the heavyhearted.

The rooms? They are found in every city in America. One is usually located on the first floor and the other somewhere off in the distance. One is called *"EMERGENCY"* and the other *"INTENSIVE."*

In one town "EMERGENCY" was located right at the front door, but "INTENSIVE" was somewhere deep within the corridors, as far away from maternity as possible. In another town "EMERGENCY" was in the back of the building by the helicopter pad, but "INTENSIVE" was five stories up and three turns away from the elevators. Every hospital has them, and few are the people who avoid them.

Faces always tell the story in these rooms. Looks convey reports lips could never speak. The eyes are often strained with tears from pressure and pain; jaws are tight, silence reigns supreme.

Emergency and Intensive care, rooms filled with hurt, fear and disappointment. Families waiting and worrying. Friends holding hands and hoping for the best.

As I told you, sparse are those who can avoid these two catacombs for cliff climbers. I am not one of that number.

The corridors were brightly lit, the leaves outside were changing colors, fall had fallen. In the room labeled "Intensive," a family grappled with grief that was far too fresh for a rational response. That family was mine.

Mom met me at the door. My brother held her hand; Mother's face published the news. Eyes puffy and swollen with tears, her cheeks were tight with the pain of a woman faced with the fact that she soon would become a widow. Few words were spoken. My little mother just fell into my arms and wept. My wife stayed close to my side, knowing when Mom sobbed, I would be next.

Everything seemed to be moving in slow motion. Somewhere in this time warp, I muttered, "Can I see him?" My brother (older by 7 years), with broken words and weeping, said, "Yes, but maybe I should go along." Mom came, too. Susan (my wife) stayed close. She knows me too well; when those I love hurt, I sometimes go to pieces.

Intensive? The worst I have ever known. Struggling? This was a new entry in my thesaurus of pain. The extension of a stroke had spiraled my dad into the "dark night of the soul" called death.

The waiting went on for two days and two nights. We had our own private family room. Tom came. He was Dad's preacher friend. They had been friends for years. I focused intently as Tom, a veteran minister, watched over the wounded. He didn't say much, just hugged my mom and told her that Irene had made some food, and that he had dropped it by the house. He looked at us and said, "I'm sorry. I loved your father. If I can be of any help, I hope you will call on me." Soothing words for some unsettled souls. Intense? The most I've ever experienced. Struggling? Now it was with my own stuff.

I learned we all must climb a few cliffs if we are to conquer. When I am climbing, a tale from a toddler gives me a new grip.

The story is told of a young boy who was taking his sister for a hike up a mountain pass, or better yet, a mountain path. As they were going along, she said, "This isn't a path. This is just a bunch of rocks and bumps." It was then that he came back with a classic line, "The bumps are what you climb on." How many of you have found that the path of life is nothing but rocks and bumps? Have you found that life is seldom even and scarcely easy? There are always rocks and bumps that cause some to climb and some to quit.

Emergency and Intensive are two bumps that every cliff climber will have to combat. Have you been there lately? Are you there now? If you are, cling to the character of God. Though you don't understand what is going on around you, God is still good and powerful. What you don't understand, he does. The bumps are what you climb on.

THE FIRST NOTE IN A SYMPHONY
FOR THE SOUL

"The Lord appeared to Joseph and said: "Don't be afraid to take Mary as your wife, for what is conceived in her is of the Holy Ghost." Matthew 1:20

"Silent night, Holy night, All is calm, All is bright." That very melody conducts a symphony within our souls. Strong sopranos, blending with finely tuned tenors. Skillful altos in line with beautiful basses. Harmony at the holidays. Melodies about the manger. We listen, and our hearts are soothed.

But what if just one of those finely tuned tenors hit a note that is sour and sickening? Harmony is hurt, and the symphony gets sacrificed. That is exactly what happened to Joseph, the husband to be of the Virgin Mary. When he heard that Mary was pregnant, he said, "I will put her away privately, because I don't want her to be put to public disgrace."

A note of discord had been inserted into the melody of Joseph's social circle. Shame and embarrassment had paid a visit to his front door. He now had two choices. He could either acknowledge the misplacement in his melody, or ignore it all together. Fundamentally, it made no difference which he did, for the false note was now traveling out into space at a rate faster than a thousand feet per second. As long as time endures, as far as he was concerned there would be discord in his world.

What he was looking for was a quiet way to restore harmony to his heart. His approach? Keep it quiet. Some will know, but they will understand. His avenue of silence would leave a few with a question or two, but in time his life's melody would no longer be a strain.

Joseph was going to relieve his fear the way many of us ease ours. Hide it. Paint a pretty picture through the power of image. Stuff it, suck it up, isolate and insulate, or put on a pretty smile, when inside there are sour notes running frantically through our broken heart. Our song is stymied, and the melody has become a malady. What else was he to do? What else would you do?

Suddenly, deep in the night, as this note of discord was flying wildly through Joseph's mind, God came near. Is there any way to restore real harmony to the world? Is there any way to recapture this sour and sickening note from an out-of-tune tenor? It can be done only by someone who is able to come in from eternity and stop the note in its wild flight. But will it still be a false note? This disharmony can be destroyed on one condition only. If that note is made the first note in a brand-new melody, then it can, again, become a harmony.

This is precisely what happened when Christ was born. There had been a false note of moral discord introduced by the first man, which had infected all humanity. God could have ignored it, but it would have been a violation of justice for him to do so. What he did, therefore, was to ask a woman, representing humanity, to bear his son.

In an act of a divine miracle an angel came and appeared to Joseph in a dream and said: "Joseph, do not be afraid to take

Mary home as your wife, because what is conceived in her is of the Holy Ghost."

Joseph had surely come to a line in the song of his life's soul that sounded out of tune. But God turned what he thought to be a sour and sick note into the first note of a brand-new song, and a whole new symphony was born.

What Joseph perceived as discord was actually a new beginning. The birth of a new thing. God was moving from law to love. From the labor of legalism to the gift of grace.

Are there any off-tune tenors in your life? Notes of discord flying wildly out of control? Has your self-respect been shattered? What you perceive as a threat to your dignity may very well be the start of a whole new song. Don't be afraid. When God comes near, the note you hear can be turned into a symphony that soothes the soul.

THE FOUR LAWS OF LOYALTY

"If your brother offends you..........." Matthew 18:15

Here's how you play. Take a three-foot long tube (much like those that hold gift wrap), connect one end to a giant set of lips and the other end to a huge plastic ear. Place ten people in a circle, put the lips to your lips and the massive ear to the ear of the person sitting next to you and say a simple message. Then hand that person the contraption and tell them to pass it on until the message gets to everyone in the group. The last person to hear the message has to repeat it just the way they heard it.

In the 1970s this game was popular. It was called *"Rumor,"* and some toy company made a killing. Our whole family used to play it, and boy, was it fun! One time the message was, "Carol, Carol, you really look like a Rhoades." By the time it got around the circle it came out, "Rasmus, Rasmus, wash your dirty clothes." We practically fell on the floor laughing, it was so funny.

Rumor is an amusing family game, but when scuttlebutt affects our comrades, it doesn't make for loyal friendships! The next time somebody sidles up to you with a big plastic ear, consider the following.

There is a law I live by that goes like this: "Don't say anything about someone you won't say to them." Jesus knew that there would be times when we would all be tempted to speak harmful words out of frustration, hurt, and disappointment. In light of that, he made a way for us to express ourselves. I call it the "Four Laws of Loyalty."

LAW NUMBER ONE: "When rumors run rampant, encourage the rock thrower to go to that person privately." We will all be tempted to get our licks in from a distance, hoping that a well-placed word to the right person will find its way back to the culprit. This is risky and unrighteous. When put in that awkward position, tell the wounded to gut it out and go to the person themselves.

Unfortunately, for a plethora of different reasons, many people avoid confrontation. Jesus knew that and said, "If that person doesn't respond, take someone with you."

LAW NUMBER TWO: "Tell the rumor-runner that you will go with them." I have often said to people, "I know the person you are speaking of, and I am sure they would want to hear what you are saying."

Sad to say, many times people just can't muster up the courage to face their fears. At this time, I point to:

LAW NUMBER THREE: "Put your frustrations on paper." Promise the frustrated one that you will personally see to it that the person who has caused their pain reads their words; in the light they have shared them. Many times, this is an effective way of helping someone solve their sticky spots.

You would hope by now that those with wagging tongues would know that your ears are not lids for a garbage can, designed to collect refuge conveniently deposited in their receptacle of choice. If these three laws fail,

LAW NUMBER FOUR is all you have left. "Leave the rumor right where you heard it." Tell the grinder at the gossip mill "if it isn't important enough for them to go to the person yourself, it's not important enough for me to repeat it."

A loyal friend is a valued investment. Cherish these simple laws, and you won't be left with, "Rasmus, washing those dirty clothes."

SIX LEGS AND LAUGHTER

I Corinthians 13:13: "But the greatest of these is love!"

Have you ever seen a man in a trench coat with six legs? A nurse at a VA hospital did.

It all started as a young man. He was a carpenter at heart, but a laborer by trade. His job? Grinding brake linings in an auto parts manufacturing plant. Not exactly his passion, but it brought in the bread and fed the babies. While his hands were grinding asbestos lined parts, his mind was envisioning finely crafted cabinets of cherry, oak, ash and maple. He was a hardwood connoisseur. Pine was for construction; hardwoods were for custom cabinets, his passion.

Years later he lived his dream: he built kitchens. Not just any kitchens, custom kitchens. Why, one kitchen was so nice a photo of it made it into a national magazine. He was good! Really good. Don't check the archives, you won't find him there. He wasn't famous, just a man with a knack for wood and a fondness for fine furnishings.

For years he was just like you and me. Got up early, read the paper and his Bible. Dressed in those blue work pants and shirt that he bought at Sears, then filled his thermos full of black coffee and out the door he went. Until one day he got the flu. Nothing unusual, we all get the flu. He coughed, sometimes heavy and hurtful. But it was just the flu.

He kept working. That's what people from his generation did. Sickness on a grand scale was never in his thinking. He tried hot tea, hot soup, expectorants and all the normal things that we fellow sufferers have downed in our times of influenza. One day it had gone on long enough. Time to see a doctor; this cold just wasn't taking flight. "Breath in, breath out," the doctor said. "Your lungs are a little congested. We'll take an X-ray." Within days a cough became cancer—asbestosis. Asbestos from grinding brake linings had found its way to his lungs, and now he had a fatal disease. Mesothelioma was not his closest companion.

Not much changed for a while. The cough hung on and became gradually worse, yet many a kitchen was still touched by the hands of this master carpenter. Sadly, there was no cure. Eventually, this dreaded disease would slowly but surely take his life. The concluding scene was on the third floor of the Veteran's Hospital. A ward, not a room.

It was in the final days that the man in the trench coat stopped to see the finest craftsman he had ever known. The clerk at the desk stopped him and said: "Where are you going?" "To the third floor to visit," came the response. "No children!" came the curt reply. The visitor smiled, leaned over and whispered, "It's their grandpa. He's real sick. I mean real sick (he didn't want to use the die word). What do ya' think? Can we get 'em in?"

"If you can get them there without anyone seeing them, have at it," the clerk responded.

Their daddy looked down at the two preschoolers and said: "You guys each grab a leg. Every time I step, you step." He then wrapped the coat around them and headed for the elevator. A man in a trench coat with six legs. They boarded what they hoped would be an express to the third floor. The little ones were laughing and fidgeting and making far too much noise, but they were all alone. It was OK. To the dismay of the father, at the second floor the elevator stopped, the door opened slowly, and in came the meanest-looking nurse in all of nurse-dom. She looked at the twenty-something man (whose heart began to pound like a jackhammer), gazed down at his legs and said, "Never seen a man with six legs before. Must be real hard keeping them all going in the same direction." Then she smiled. "Where are you going, sir?" She asked. "Third floor," the nervous father responded. "That's where I'm going," came her response. Just then a girlish giggle came from under the coat. The nurse just smiled and asked, "Who you going to see?" "Ah, Ed, ah, Ed Lobley," the father chortled. "I'll take you right to him," the now-not-so-mean looking nurse replied.

Off they went, past nurse's stations and custodians, who were all snickering at the young father with six legs. Into the ward they shuffled. The over coat was opened and out popped a blonde boy and a brunette girl. "Hi Grandpa!" They giggled.

"How did you guys get in here?" He asked through gasps for air. "Children aren't allowed on this floor." They told him the whole story and then said something that made his thin face flinch to hold back tears. "We snuck up under Dad's coat because we love you, and we wanted to see you!"

A few days later, my father-in-law, one of the finest finish men the carpenter's world has ever known succumbed to cancer. That six-legged journey was the last time my children got to be tickled and teased by Grandpa. All because they loved him.

What journey do you need to make to show your love? It might just be a trip down the hall to a child's bedroom to kiss a sleeping cheek. Or maybe a stroll to the lady loading the dishwasher to share a hug and a thank you. It might cost you a plane ticket, a bus ticket, three hours in a car, or it may only necessitate a little sneak to the third floor.

By the way, if you see a man in a trench coat with six legs, don't be concerned. It's just some dad with his kid's going to the third floor to visit Grandpa!

WRONG NOTE, RIGHT TIME

Joshua 4:7 "These stones are to be a memorial to the people of Israel forever."

Don't ever start the Star-Spangled Banner in the wrong key! Francis Scott Key would have held his ears the last time I did. On July 27th, 1994 (the hottest day of the year), I was asked to sing the great song that honors our flag. At the end of a parade commemorating Armistice day, a crowd of several hundred gathered in the driveway of the local VFW hall where speeches were made, and I was called upon to sing the national anthem.

As the first "Oh say" passed through my lips, I knew that I was heading to notes that were an octave out of my range. By the time I arrived at "the rockets' red glare," the veins in my head were "bursting in air." I was literally screaming to try and reach the high notes. My version sounded a lot like Alfalfa in The Little Rascals. You can only imagine how horrible I sounded and how terrible I felt. After I finished the final line I was glad to be "free" and not quite sure if I was "brave" enough to ever sing our nation's song in public again.

I tried hard to slip into the crowd unnoticed, hoping to get to my car without crossing paths with a veteran. I just wanted to go home. What happened next renewed my hope that there were better times ahead.

As I hastily made my way to the car, an older man, well into his sixties, laid his hand on my shoulder, stopping me in my tracks. As I sheepishly looked up at the tall, gray-haired fellow, he had huge tears in his eyes. He looked down at me and said, "Reverend, I want you to know that was the best I have ever heard anyone sing the national anthem." What could I say? He was either lying or deaf. In my ears that was the worst I had ever heard anyone sing that powerful song. He said one more thing that remains etched in the granite of my soul. "I fought in the Korean War, and saw many of my fellow soldiers die. Every time I hear those words and see that flag, I cry like a child. You warmed my heart today. Thanks for taking your time and coming to our parade. You sure are a great singer."

I thanked him, knowing full well that his exposure to great singers was severely limited. As I rode home, I made a pact that I would turn down any future opportunity to do acappella projects. I kept that promise for several years.

It wasn't until the winter of 1995 that I sang the national anthem again in public. I was standing in the middle of a wrestling mat preparing to officiate a high school wrestling match. The athletic director asked the crowd to rise and honor our country. He pressed the button to play a Whitney Houston CD, and it just wouldn't play. He pressed it again, and still nothing. You could hear the ripple of nervous laughter roll through the crowd as he said, "Well, I'm not going to sing it. I guess we'll just have to go without it tonight."

I had a flashback to that driveway and the encounter with my tone-deaf friend. My heart said, "You sing it." Without hesitation I looked at the school official and said, "May I have the microphone? I'll sing it." He looked at me and said, "Have at it." I let it rip. Right key. Right place. Right time. I don't know whether it was for my reffing or my singing, but from that night on I officiated at least one home match at that school every season. They always asked me to sing the nation's song. I always obliged.

The sincere words of a tall, gray-haired veteran helped me realize that notes weren't the only thing that moves a heart. It's the memories. I gained a new appreciation for those who served this nation, especially the ones who gave their lives. I am forever grateful for the tenderhearted soldier who took his time to mend my mistake and give patriotism a seat in my soul. He helped me understand the statement of the ancients that said, "Tell the next generation what these stones mean."

WITHOUT A RECIPE, WE RISK REMORSE

A wise old man once said: "Trust in the Lord with all your heart, and lean not on your own understanding. In all your ways acknowledge him, and he will make your paths straight." (Proverbs 3:5-6). STRAIGHT PATHS! Who wouldn't want a life like that? Just how do you get life to straighten out? It seems that Solomon gave us a recipe, and recipes are important.

I LOVE TO COOK! Ever since I was a child, I enjoyed learning how to make my own food. The older I got, the more I learned. There was a time in my life that I actually set my sights on becoming a chef.

For a long time, however, I didn't think it manly to use a cookbook. That was just for those with less insight into the world of "parsley, sage, rosemary and thyme." It was a one-year-old that finally taught me that my love of food and my craving for the zesty side of flavor was not for everyone.

While I was attending college full-time and working part-time at three jobs, my wife worked full-time. Quite often it was my responsibility to cook supper. I loved serving spaghetti. The sauce and meatballs were fun to make, and it was even more fun to watch our one-year-old son try to negotiate noodles and sauce from a bowl to his mouth. I looked forward to long sessions of Brandon covered from head to toe with Daddy's seasoned sauce fit for "Luciano Pavarotti."

One night when Susan arrived home from work, Brandon was in the high chair, and the floor was covered with paper (for protection from his wild child antics with "sabetti"). I dished him out a bowl full of fine nutrition, and he was off to the races. There were noodles stuck to his face and hair, and he had sauce in places that only a good bath could eliminate. Several minutes into his meal, long before we got a chance to sit down, he began to cry and say, "hot, Daddy, hot." I knew it couldn't be too hot, but I touched it to my lips and said, "No, sweetheart, it's not too hot. It has cooled long enough. You can go ahead and eat." Susan and I sat down to eat our share of Italian fixens', when he started again. "Hot, Daddy, hot." I assured him that it was "OK," that it was plenty cool, and he would be fine.

It was now Susan's turn to dig into my concoction of sauce and spices. Her eyes began to water, face began to turn red, and suddenly she was backstroking her way out of this banquet gone blistering. "Stephen, this is incredibly hot. What did you put in this?" I responded, "Crushed red pepper, a little cayenne and some Frank's Durkee's Red Hot Sauce—but not much." "Have you tasted it?" she asked. "Yeah, but it doesn't seem hot to me." At that point, Brandon had stopped his journey down the path of fiery food and was just saying, "hot, Daddy, hot." I then tried a heaping helping of my own hospitality. Let me tell you, this was some of the hottest stuff I had ever let pass my lips. It was not fit for a one-year-old to digest. In fact, this wasn't fit for an "any-year-old" to eat. This was "steam city." I learned something from that moment of culinary disaster. "When there is no recipe, you risk regret." My "sabetti" went down the garbage disposal.

Recipes are essential when trying to avoid regret. Wise old Solomon gave us one that will never leave us saying, "hot, Daddy, hot." Do you want straight paths? Trust... and follow the recipe.

WRECKED, BUT NOT RUINED

ROMANS 12:14: "Bless those who persecute you, bless and do not curse."

My first real car was not a car at all. It was a truck. A 1967 G.M.C. pickup truck. The first time I saw it I had feelings of disappointment and hopelessness. My brother-in-law made a statement that will stick with me for the rest of my life........... "DON'T LOOK AT IT FOR WHAT IT IS NOW, BUT FOR WHAT IT CAN BECOME." Over the next several months we turned that finger-painted primer mobile to a "MEAN GREEN MUSIC MACHINE."

When we finally finished the truck, I enjoyed summer rides down Kirkwood Highway with my girlfriend, Susan (now my wife). We listened to the top 40 on my 8-track player, relishing every moment as people at red lights stared at the fruit of my labor. There was just something about that old truck that made me feel good. In the morning, I couldn't wait to drive it. On the weekends, I couldn't wait to wash it; and when people would come close to it, I couldn't stand to have them mess with it. It was finished, and it needed to be protected. I would guard it scrupulously. I was going to preserve this machine, and I did everything I could to see that nothing would soil its fine design. But that was soon to change.

One fall day when the leaves were just beginning to come to their peak colors, I was driving down the back roads of Yorklyn, Pa. My friend Ben and I were returning from a football game.

The music was playing (I think it was James Taylor's "Rock-a-bye Sweet Baby James), and the weather was beautiful. THAT IS WHEN IT HAPPENED! As I was approaching the bottom of the hill and stopping for the intersection's stop sign, some 16-year-old in his mother's car was going too fast, hit his breaks, and skidded out of control into the left front corner panel of my "MEAN GREEN MUSIC MACHINE." That was "THE DAY THE MUSIC DIED." I could hear the metal crunch and see the shattered glass go flying across the intersection as we felt the impact. My heart sank, and my temperature rose. As I went to open the door, it sounded like the back door on our shed out in the yard. CreeeeeK!!!!! And then there was the "POP!!!!!" of the metal corner panel unlocking itself from the passenger door. I actually had to kick it open. I checked on the driver of the other car. He was all right. I checked on Ben; he was fine. Time now to survey the damage. I CRIED. "REAL TEARS!" The truck was smashed. Ruined? No! Wrecked? Yes! It was then I learned a valuable lesson.

"NO MATTER HOW HARD YOU TRY, YOU'RE GOING TO GET BROADSIDED!" You can't avoid it. You can't block it out. Sometime, someplace, you will meet with someone's child driver. They will lose control, and you will find yourself pushing open the door, finding out if everyone is OK, and then staring at broken parts, shattered glass, cracked paint, and a dream gone to demolition.

As I stood at that intersection waiting for the police to arrive, I was already deciding. What should I do with the truck? This accident wasn't my fault. I was just plain innocent. I was hit broadside, and my belief in restoration was facing the test of resiliency. What was I going to do? Determine it was a wreck to be restored, or a waste declared ruined? Restoration was hard, but it was right. To bless when you've been burnt isn't easy.

Here's one for ya. "She has every reason to be bitter. Though talented, she went unrecognized for years. Prestigious opera circles closed their ranks when she tried to enter. American critics ignored her compelling voice. She was repeatedly rejected for parts for which she was easily qualified. It was only after she went to Europe and won the hearts of the tough to please European audiences, that stateside opinion leaders acknowledged her talent.

Not only has her professional life been a battle, but her personal life was also marked by challenge. She is the mother of two handicapped children, one of whom is severely retarded. Years ago, in order to escape the pace of New York City, she purchased a home on Martha's Vineyard. It burned to the ground two days before she was to move in."

Professional rejection. Personal setbacks. Perfect soil for seeds of bitterness. A receptive field for the roots of resentment. But in this case, anger knocked and found no one home.

Her friends don't call her bitter; they call her "Bubbles."

Beverly Sills. Internationally acclaimed opera singer. Retired director of the New York City Opera.

Her phrases are sugared with laughter. Her face is softened with serenity. Upon interviewing her, Mike Wallace stated, "she is one of the most impressive—if not *the* most impressive—ladies I've ever interviewed."

How can a person handle such professional rejection and personal trauma and still be known as Bubbles? "I choose to be cheerful," she says. "Years ago, I knew I had little or no choice about success, circumstances or even unhappiness; but I knew I could choose to be cheerful."

Have you been broadsided or betrayed lately? Are you wrecked or ruined? Amidst the broken glass or tested career, will you be known as bitter or Bubbles?

YOU DA BEST

"As a man thinks in his heart, so is he!" Proverbs 23:7 KJV

Our son, the oldest child, is a graduate of Harvard. Our oldest daughter, a junior at The University of Pennsylvania, and our youngest, a seventh grader. From the day they entered school, I promised Brandon, Erin and Allison I would drive them there every morning. That was a grand idea when Brandon entered kindergarten; the elementary school was three miles from our house. I kept my promise until we moved to a smaller town. When we arrived, my wife asked, "What are you going to do with your driving promise now that we live a whopping 200 yards from the doors to the school?"

With fearless resolve, I stated, "I am going to drive them." Every school day for the five years we lived there, off we rode each morning. That practice continues to this day, and we live less than a block from Allie's elementary school.

I wanted my children to start their day with the last words they heard before entering the school doors to come from Dad. For many years I always said the same thing. "Did you do you do your homework?" A little late for a remedy, but I knew that "observed behavior changes." There were few times the answer was "No."

Eventually, the final words changed. Allie and I would drive the eighteen seconds it took to get to school, and in the process have a few routines that became habit forming. We can't leave the driveway without the seat belt buckled. She quotes the crash dummies as the belt clicks around her waist: "Always buckle up, no matter how short the trip. Most accidents happen with three miles of your house."

We would then trek up the block; and just as I am dropping her off, she slips her backpack over her shoulder, grabs her lunchbox, climbs out the door and slowly pushes it almost closed. She peaks her head right up to the crack and says as quickly as she can, "You da best!" I try to beat her, because the last one to say it wins. I usually pull off the upset when I simply crack the electric window and yell, "You da best," then push the close button, making me champion until tomorrow.

In April of 2000, I couldn't drive Allison to school. I had come down with pneumonia. The couch had become my constant companion, and my doctor said, "stay in bed, or the next stop will be Regional Hospital." On the first morning I couldn't make the drive, Allison kissed me goodbye in the family room and walked to the top of the steps. She stepped outside the storm door, got it almost shut, peaked her nose inside the crack and shouted loud enough for me to hear, "You da best!" and off she ran.

That's not fair! I'm dying! I couldn't stand it. I crawled off the sofa, drug myself to the window, and threw open the sash. Just before she could flee the confines of our backyard through the big wooden gate, I screamed, "NO, you da best!" I won again!!!!

Now I know that not everyone will agree that my children are the best. But that doesn't change how I feel about them. In my eyes they are and will always be the best.

Jesus, to the chagrin of his disciples, brought the little ones unto himself and placed his hands on them and "blessed them." We can learn a lot from that brief Bible lesson. The spoken message has great affect. "You Da Best!"

A LESSON CONCERNING LEAVING

NEHEMIAH 2:4 "THEN I PRAYED TO THE GOD OF HEAVEN, AND I ANSWERED THE KING, "IF IT PLEASES THE KING AND IF YOUR SERVANT HAS FOUND FAVOR IN HIS SIGHT, LET HIM SEND ME TO THE CITY IN JUDAH WHERE MY FATHERS ARE BURIED SO THAT I CAN REBUILD IT."

This is a lesson on leaving!

Winter storms are no surprise on the west side of the Missouri river. Sudden snow squalls of several inches can appear out of nowhere in seconds. When the wind and weather produce blowing and snowing, life gets slippery. That was the case for a twenty-one-year-old girl who will remain nameless.

She was on her way to the airport early on a Thursday morning to feed the customers at her waitressing job in the coffee shop. About a mile from the entrance, as snow and wind blinded the highway, her compact car crossed the center line of the two-lane and smashed head on into an oncoming snow plow, who never saw her coming. She survived, and I got the phone call to come to the ICU.

Upon arrival, the attending surgeon, (a friend of mine) told me that he had looked at the x-rays and to the best of his ability he could not find one major bone in her body that wasn't broken. She wasn't going to make it, but they would do all they could to keep her alive until her mother could arrive from Nebraska.

I waited in the little room off the ICU, which had a sign on the door that read..." family only." But there was no family, just myself and a couple of loosely connected friends who began pouring endless questions into an empty bucket of answers.

From time to time the nurse would peek in to see if our friends' mother had arrived, but with the traffic outside moving like thick molasses it would be awhile.

The silence of that little room was almost eerie. Tick-tock, tick tock, the ten-inch circle chimed. Time was clicking off and quiet was our only companion.

After a couple of hours, in walked a weeping mother. She had very little information on her daughter's condition, simply that she had been seriously hurt. She looked straight at me and said, "How bad is she?" My expression spread the news. I didn't say a word, she collapsed into my arms. I whispered in her ear, what the doctor had told me, which produced a wail of sobbing. "Can she talk to me?" The brokenhearted mother asked. "No." I replied, but she may be able to hear you. I prepared her for what she was about to see and slowly we wandered behind the curtain.

No words can describe the agony I saw and heard that day. The first words her mother spoke seemed odd, "I'm sorry," mom said. "I'm so sorry. I wish things had ended differently." Needless to say I was a little confused, but when you witness shock, there are no surprises.

We stayed for a while. I stood awkwardly off to the side waiting to escort mom back to that little room. As I was leaving, my friend, the surgeon said, "We're going to turn off the machine, and it will only be a matter of minutes." It was and then raw reality met a wrecked relationship.

In less than a half an hour the nurse came and relayed the report, she was gone. Mom asked everyone to leave but me. I stayed quietly in my seat and watched as a devastated mother stumbled through a veil of tears and said, "I don't know how I will handle this, the last thing we did was fight. We screamed at each other and I said, "I'm leaving," I grabbed my stuff, threw it in some nylon bags and moved to Nebraska. That was 5 months ago and we haven't spoken since. How am I going to live with that the rest of my life with these feelings of guilt?"

What could I say? What would you say? I didn't say much. "I believe God knows how much you loved her, he will help you." Was all I could muster. It seemed so shallow, but what else is there at a time like that. It was all so final. No words of mine were going to rearrange this confusion.

Leaving and life have an odd way of intersecting. Sometimes it's fruitful and other times it's faulty. Parting should be a process, not a huff and a puff and a nylon bag full of nothing.

Do you have any departures on the horizon? Put away the nylon bags and settle your strains, it will save you a bundle of bulging bags.

ALERT, BUT NOT ALARMED

Acrophobia? Agoraphobia? Algophobia? Arachnophobia? Brontophobia? Lygophobia? Panophobia? You may not recognize the first half of these words, but most likely you are familiar with the second. From heights, open spaces, crowded places, pain, spiders, thunder, lightning, and darkness, to the fear of everything. Phobias affect us all! Everybody fears something. Even Superman was afraid of kryptonite.

Jesus understood this fact. However, He was concerned that we not become focused on our fears. One time He said to His disciples, "I have told you these things so that in me you will have peace. In this world you will have trouble (tight spots, pressing pressures, fears), but be of good cheer, I have overcome the world" (John 16:33).

Several months ago a friend of mine was speaking in New York City. The church he preached in had bars on the windows, and the people had every reason to be concerned about the environment. My friend asked the pastor how he handled the concerns of the congregation. The inner-city pastor responded: "It's really no problem. We live by the code: "be alert, but don't be alarmed!" I will always remember that. It makes sense.

This principle became reality in my life 13 years ago. "There are cracks in that dock, Dad. I can see the water down below." Those were the words of a five-year-old that was quite concerned about walking on water, even though there was a dock to keep him dry. But when you've almost drowned twice in your first five years of life, water takes on a whole new meaning. Instead of splashing and swimming, you feel paralysis and panic.

As I walked with my pre-school child along a perfectly safe dock in Baltimore, Maryland, I realized that as his father it was going to be up to me to make sure he had a healthy fear of water. I stooped down to his level, looked him right in the eye and said, "those two times you almost drowned still scare you, don't they?" "Yeah," he replied. We ventured on. As we walked slowly out to the boats, there was still a little tremble in his step; but he got over the fear, and we enjoyed the boats. Anxious? Yes. Panicked? No. By the way, this past summer he caught a fifty-pound Tuna fish, 47 miles out into the Atlantic Ocean.

That moment brought back the old principle I learned several years ago: *"SHEEP SCATTER SHEEP, SHEPHERDS SETTLE SHEEP."* Loving leaders make sure we know there will be pain, but they don't push the panic button every time there are cracks in the walkway. Paul told Timothy, "God has not given us the spirit of fear, but of power, love and a sound mind."

> Overcoming fear is found when you meet the man who proclaimed that he was the "Good Shepherd." His name is Jesus. He hasn't come to scatter the Sheep by filling their lives with panic. He has come to settle the Sheep by bringing peace. The next time your phobias kick in, remember the "Good Shepherd" is with you. Be alert, but not alarmed!

DO GOOD! THE DAYS ARE SHORT!

JAMES 4:13-17 "Life is a vapor...and he who knows the good he ought to do and doesn't do it, sins."

The last thing I did with Jeff was laugh, and the last thing I did with Paul was kick shots to his wide side to make him a better goalie.

The two-mile bus trip was filled with the usual laughter and shenanigans of tenth graders. But when we got to the field, it was all business. "Big arm circles, now little arm circles," hollered out the captain of the McKean High School J.V. baseball team. About that time, I heard a soft whisper from my left say almost silently, "Hey Rhoadsie, I can't see." I whispered back to our burly first baseman, Jeff Booth. He was good...really good. "Quit complaining, man. These are easy." "I think I'm going to pass out," he whispered back. I just chuckled a little and said: "Stop talking, or we're going to get in trouble." But he wasn't kidding. The next thing I knew Jeff collapsed in a heap on the freshly mowed spring Delaware grass. The coach and several players gathered over him. Within moments they moved us all away, instructing us to "play some pepper."

I kept one eye on the half swinging pepper player, and the other on my friend, Jeff. I saw Coach Miller start to cry and slap his hands on his thighs in a panic. It was before cell phones, so someone had to run to the Sanford School gym and call an ambulance. In a few minutes, you could hear the sirens in the background coming up Newport Gap Pike. Into the parking lot they raced, loaded up our clean-up hitter; and, just as quickly, they were off.

Coach didn't say much when we asked him what was wrong. He just said, "We'll wait to hear." Then he left and went to the hospital. We played that game not knowing that one of our best friends had died instantly of a cerebral hemorrhage. In the twinkle of an eye, a fifteen-year-old was gone!

Funerals weren't meant for sophomores, but three days later thirty of us, dressed in baseball jerseys, lined the pews of a local church. It didn't seem real, but real it was. And that reality remained alive every time we suited up. For the rest of the season we wore black patches on our jersey sleeves, with number 15 stitched inside, a small reminder of a life gone way too early.

A year and a half had passed since that tragic and confusing period in my young life. I moved to a new school and joined the soccer team. I was in my senior year and enjoying the pre-season, playing mid-field for the Alexis I. DuPont Tigers. One of the greatest assets on that team was our goalie, Paul Keispert—6'3" tall with hands like velcro and feet like Baryshnikov. He was already penned in as an All-State Net-Minder. Man, was he good and a whole lot humble.

As I remember it, about two weeks into the pre-season he took a hard shot off his right forearm causing it to quickly swell up like a balloon. Coach Timmeny pulled him off the practice field, wrapped it in ice and sent him home with his mom to see a doctor. Paul didn't come to school the next day. In fact, he never returned to school at all. It was discovered that he had a rapid moving cancer, and shortly thereafter, he died, a 17-year-old soccer star with an all-state trophy waiting, gone.

I attended my second funeral in less than two years. Sitting in the fourth row of an Episcopal church, I suddenly didn't feel so invincible. For the next few months, the thought of being an indestructible adolescent ran head-on into the reality of the brevity of life. Both of these guys were not only good athletes, but they were good people. Kind, considerate and both had their ego's in check.

None of us are assured of tomorrow. James knew that, and he used that fact as a basis for a glimpse at living each day to the fullest.

He borrowed a phrase from the ancient warrior Job, as he painted this picture of this pressing issue called death. Job gives us a glimpse of the seriousness of life and death. "*The cloud is consumed and vanishes away*" (Job 7:9). We count our years at each birthday, but God tells us to number our days (Psalm 90:12).

At the time of this writing I have lived over 15,000 days. Each one of them has offered thousands of opportunities to "do good." I lament the fact that I have let so many of those "good" opportunities pass me by. Life is but a vapor. It is here today and gone tomorrow. Have you missed any opportunities to "be good" lately? Go for it, someone will remember.

FOR A KEYCHAIN?

"I have fought the good fight, I have finished the race, I have kept the faith. Now there is in store for me a crown of righteousness, which the Lord, the righteous judge, will award me on that day."
(II Timothy 4:7-80).

Nestled in the patchwork quilt-colored hills of the Susquehanna Valley in northeast Pennsylvania, each Thanksgiving there is a race. It's not a marathon, not even a half marathon. If I remember correctly, it is 9.6 miles of rolling foliage and rugged hills. In 1985, the "Run for the Diamonds" celebrated its 75th anniversary. In normal years the race promoters gave every registered runner a free T-shirt just for entering, but that year every finisher received a commemorative brass key chain.

When the newspaper announced that each finisher would collect more than just a T-shirt, I couldn't resist. I was never much on running long distances. In my opinion, anything longer than 400 meters is cruel and unusual punishment. On this day I banished that thought, stepped outside my comfort zone and tackled this footrace through the foothills.

My first challenge was what to wear. Not being a "real" runner, my wardrobe wasn't stocked with the fineries of spandex Adidas leggings, running shorts, nor a fancy brightly colored shirt. I wore soccer shorts and a T-shirt that said, "POWER" in big letters and the words "I can do all things through Christ" scripted underneath. Fitting apparel for a preacher with one thing on his mind: finishing!

Eleven hundred runners came to run that day. Most of them were running for a chance at the diamond rings that were awarded for the first two places. I came for a key chain, nothing more, and certainly nothing less! We all gathered at the corner of First and Market, 100 yards from the Susquehanna River. The gun sounded and off we went, up Market Street for a mile.

The river of runners snaked out of town. Friends told me I should practice on the course, but I never found the time. It wasn't very long before I realized that I should have listened. The first three miles of this course were all uphill. Not steep, just grimly gradual. Just as my lungs began to burn and my brain began to bargain with my body, a young girl came flying by and said, "Guess your gonna need two of those power shirts today, huh?" She wasn't a little child; she was old enough to know better than to insult a wheezing geezer!

I was offended and immediately spoke back to my brain, "We will finish!!" The next two miles were flat and gradually down-hill. I had numerous arguments with my lungs and legs for the next hour, but I just kept placing one aching foot in front of the other. Five miles, six, seven and then eight. About this time. I came upon that same young girl who had insulted me on my first uphill grind. I still had a mile to go, but I felt a rush of adrenaline like I had never experienced before. I was almost in a full sprint when I caught and passed her. What would I say as I whizzed by? I decided it would be just enough to slow down long enough for her to have to read my shirt just one more time. Anyway, I didn't need to say anything. I wasn't running this race for her; I was running it for the key-chain.

A few minutes later I finished the race, zigzagged my way through the awards line, got my time and place (none of your business), and was handed my brass key-chain. To this day I still haven't used it. It means something to me. I finished. I didn't win. I didn't even come close, but I finished. Not only that, but I won the prize. FINISH! There's a prize that's waiting.

GET ME TO THE CONCERT ON TIME

Luke 19:32 . . . Those that owned the colt said:
"why are you untying the colt?"

Rahab used a rope, Paul's rope holders used a basket, David used a sling, Samson used a jawbone, Moses used a stick, Mary gave perfume, four friends used a mat, Peter and John only had their words and some real hot faith, Ruth used her heart of commitment and loyalties, the widow gave two small coins, and Larry used a wrench.

Two thousand years ago an unnamed man was asked to let the master use his colt. Two thousand years later, God wants to know if he can use yours. My what? You may ask. Your donkey. We all have one, you know.

It was over forty years ago, and I was traveling in southern New Jersey on my way to Atlantic City to do a gospel concert with my family. About 20 miles from the church we dropped our drive shaft from the bus. The mechanic among us mentioned something about a universal joint????? Oh, I don't know. But anyway, the part was lying on the ground, and we were in big trouble. We weren't late yet; but if we didn't get this thing fixed, the whole night would be ruined, and we would have to cancel. To add to this already discouraging news, we were stuck in the middle of a pouring rainstorm. The shoulder of the road had become flooded like a Southern Texas gully in a hurried hurricane.

I didn't have a clue what we were going to do. Just when all of us non-mechanic types were ready to panic, my brother-in-law Larry said, "Give me a blanket." He crawled under the bus and looked over the situation. He came back to the front door, got on the CB and called out on channel 19. It went something like this: "Hey, hey, good buddy. We're broken down on the Atlantic City Expressway and need a universal for a 1972 Chevy school bus. If you can find me a mechanic, it sure would help." Back came a voice: "I am the mechanic. I'm sitting here in my parts store, and if you can get me the right numbers, I can get it right out to you." One hour and one severely soaked set of clothes later, the pit crew boss of the Rhoades family had that old school bus ready, and back on the road and just in time for the concert. Now, that's what I call service.

But what if my brother-in-law would have said: "It's too wet. What's one concert? I know I can fix it, but I'm not going to get involved. I'll just keep my mouth shut and wait till the rain stops, and we can get a tow truck."

We would have all survived, but we would have lost something, and so would he. We would have lost an opportunity to sing, and he would have lost the opportunity to serve.

Opportunity knocked and a gifted car man got generous.

My Brother-in-law is just one guy in a long line of good people, who gave little things to the people he loved the most.

What opportunity is knocking at your door? Who knows, you just may be the one who will get us all to the concert on time.

LET GO OF THE ROPE?

II TIMOTHY 2:1-10 "Endure hardship with us like a good soldier of Jesus Christ."

Head-first slides into second base are not recommended for 41-year-olds who have long since passed their prime! I should know. The last time I tried it, I ended up with 5 stitches that reconnected my pinkie finger to its original owner. It hurt!

Have you ever wished you just didn't have to feel pain? That the hard road of hardship never docked at your port? We have all wished we could go through life without being hurt, and that we would just be better off if we could feel no pain. Although that sounds good, in reality it probably wouldn't be so good. Listen to the following illustration given by Charles Swindoll in his book, "Steadfast Christianity," regarding pain.

Approximately one out of every 400,000 babies will live a short, tragic life due to a rare genetic disease known as familial dysautonomia. This disease prevents a child from feeling pain. At first reflection, this seems a blessing. Imagine the possibilities-a football player who doesn't feel the pain of contact; a boxer who can endure a terrible beating in the ring and not feel the hurt; a woman who can bear children without the pain of childbirth. The tragedy is that a child with this disease will never live long enough to know the glory of the gridiron or the joy of childbirth. Such a child will receive cuts, burns and broken bones-never feeling anything. A cavity will rot the tooth without an ache. A broken bone will puncture the skin before anyone is aware of a fracture. An appendix will burst without a sharp pain in the side. Pain can be good. It can be God's warning device that something is wrong-like the red light on the dashboard that alerts you to the fact that the engine is hot, or the battery is low or the oil pressure is dropping. Pain often seems pointless, but we are assured by God that it is always purposeful."

Paul specifically addresses the issue of pain with his protégé preacher, Timothy. It was important for Timothy to learn young that afflictions are a part of life, and that hard times quite often are the cause of a hard heart..

If pain is inescapable, and hard hearts are to be avoided, then how can we find relief?

The story is told of a man who was walking along a steep cliff. He slipped and fell to what appeared to be his doom. As he was sliding, he grabbed a branch as it whisked by his ear and hung on in panic. As he squeezed for his life he screamed, "Is there anybody up there? Help me!" A voice came back and said: "This is God. I can help you, let go of the rope!" To which the man replied, "Is there anybody else up there?"

When we're in pain, we need relief now. Mine came in the form of a graduate of the University of Iowa who had gone on to become an emergency room doctor. For many it will come in prayer from the end of a branch. Either way, at some point you are going to have to let go of the rope, accept the pain and look for relief.

Has pain affected your heart? Have hard times sent you reeling? Are you docked in the port of hard knocks, yearning for a case of the numbs? Scripture teaches us that pain is inevitable, but misery is an option. Jesus said: "In this world you will have troubles (pain), but be of good cheer, for I have overcome the world." Why not let go of the rope, fall into the hands of a loving savior and let him heal your pain.

By the way, when sliding, go feet first. Some hurts are meant to be avoided.

THE REMARKABLE REWARDS
OF A ROAD TRIP

"On the way, Jesus asked them, "Who do people say that I am?"
. . . . Peter finally responded by saying, "You are the Christ, the
son of the living God."

Nine states and 4038 miles in seven days. Now that's a road trip!

"It's a long fly ball, deep to left field. It's going, it's going, it's outta here! The Cubs win, the Cubs win!!!!" What a shot! Sammy Sosa's bat had collided with an unfortunate Florida Marlin's hurler's pitch, and the Cubbies' pulled one out in the bottom of the ninth, and I was there.

Not only was I there, but I watched that deep shot to the street with my one and only son. Brandon and I are on a lifelong quest to see every major league baseball park in my lifetime. Wrigley Field fit our travel plans on our recent road trip home from college. Two sweatshirts (that's a story for another time), three hot dogs and some cheese nachos later, Wrigley was checked off the list.

Just as we were leaving the stadium, I noticed on the scoreboard that the Braves were in Milwaukee that same night, and a light went on. We both agreed that there was no time like the present to check one more park off the list. County Stadium and Wrigley all in the same day. Ninety-two miles and two traffic jams later, we were in row nineteen, eating bratwurst and peanuts, watching the Braves knock off the Brewers.

I will cherish that road trip with my son for the rest of my life. We cruised through the Catskills, enjoyed Pennsylvania's rolling green hills, collected coins from the ashtray to pay those tolls through Chicago and eventually welcomed some well-deserved rest in a Sioux Falls motel. *"Along the way"* I learned a few things.

Although Jesus didn't have the benefit of a 1992 mini-van, he did take advantage of "the rewards of a road trip." The Bible speaks often of the benefits of his "along the way" journeys. "Along the way" Peter revealed his true feelings about Jesus. "Along the way" Jesus showed his concern for a man who was crippled for 38 years. The list goes on and on, revealing the merits of Jesus' "along the way" experiences. I read recently in James Dobson's book entitled, "Straight Talk," the average amount of time spent by a middle-class father with their small children was thirty-seven seconds per day! Their direct interaction was limited to 2.7 encounters daily, lasting ten to fifteen seconds each!" Unfortunately, modern man has allowed the bane of business to diminish the opportunities for "along the way" rewards.

Although I don't have a hankering for a trip like the last any time soon, I don't regret the 30 hours spent with my son. Plan an "along the way" road trip today. It's amazing what you will learn.

ACKNOWLEDGMENTS

I was born on March 22, 1957. I always say that on that day, all the alarms in heaven went off, angels and seraphim came running, everyone had gathered for something very important. God had called for an "all hands-on deck meeting." He said, "Does everyone realize that Steve was born this morning? We must make sure that within the next year, Susan must be born. If she is not, this boy will never make it." On March 7th, 1958, Susan was born, and all was right with the world. Thank you, God, for giving me Susan and thank you Susan for making sure "I made it." You are wonderful.

ABOUT THE AUTHOR

Forty years as a pastor, an All-American collegiate wrestler, fifteen years as an NCAA Soccer official, at twelve started traveling with his family singing Southern Gospel music for twelve years, recorded two albums at the famous Hilltop Studios in Nashville, Tennessee, sang on the Grand Ole Opry at age seventeen, married to Susan for forty-three years, father of three, grandfather to nine, traveled to every US state but one, spent time on four continents, and presently has eighty three people in his extended family. Steve has a story for just about everything.